HAU~~N~~

WEXFORD

HAUNTED
WEXFORD

Michael Benson

The
History
Press
Ireland

To all those people past and present who
have made and continue to make me what I am,
especially my parents, my wife Gina and my
two beautiful children, Jamie and Michael.

First published 2014

The History Press Ireland
50 City Quay
Dublin 2
Ireland
www.thehistorypress.ie

© Michael Benson, 2014
Foreword © Steve Parsons, 2014

The right of Michael Benson to be identified as the Author
of this work has been asserted in accordance with the
Copyright, Designs and Patents Act 1988.

British Library Cataloguing in Publication Data.
A catalogue record for this book is available from the British Library.

ISBN 978 1 84588 791 9

Typesetting and origination by The History Press

CONTENTS

	About the Author	7
	Acknowledgements	9
	Foreword	11
	Introduction	13
one	Who's There?	15
two	Enniscorthy Castle	18
three	Loftus Hall	29
four	The Ballymurn Case	37
five	Neighbouring Ghosts	45
six	Duncannon Fort	53
seven	St Senan's Hospital	62
eight	Enduring Spirits	66
nine	Three's a Crowd	77
ten	Mom's Cottage	81
eleven	In Wilton's Shadow	87
twelve	A Barrel of Laughs	94

ABOUT THE AUTHOR

MICHAEL Benson grew up in Wexford where he continues to live with his wife and two children. He has had an interest in the subject of the paranormal for many years and he is the founder of Wexford Paranormal.

Michael has a B.Soc.Sc degree in Social Science and this is a background that Michael feels contributes greatly on an ongoing basis to his work in this field.

Like many others who pursue a greater understanding of the subject, his interest stems from a number of experiences he had when he was younger.

He has worked for a number of years now both as an individual investigator and with his team at Wexford Paranormal. Doing so has provided him with the opportunity to perhaps better understand his own experiences while being of service to others. This also removes any emotional attachment he may have to the occurrences taking place.

Fundamental to the work that Michael and the team at Wexford Paranormal do when working on private cases is the fact that their services are provided free of charge in every instance. 'Making a positive difference is what matters; even if we can simply cause someone to positively change how they view the situation, the experience that follows often changes as well.'

In the past few years Michael has contributed to a number of radio shows both here, in the UK and America on the subject of the paranormal, and both he and the team are often sought out by students and the public alike for comment on the subject of the paranormal.

His greatest pleasure is meeting the many people whom he has worked with over the years, many of whom have become close friends along the way.

ACKNOWLEDGEMENTS

BEHIND all the places, cases and locations contained in this book are the experiences of the people involved. I would like to take this opportunity to thank all of these people for their participation, time and honesty with regard to their stories.

I also want to acknowledge the contribution, support, encouragement and council of the numerous people who have shared the many parts of this journey with me that has, over time, ultimately lead to the completion of this piece of work, this book that is *Haunted Wexford*.

I would also like to thank the editor and staff of The History Press Ireland for their guidance and advice – as well as their unending patience in answering my many questions – in bringing all the various elements of this book together.

To John McNicholas, my English teacher, who ignited in me a passion for the magic of the written word over thirty years ago.

Finally to you the reader, who, with every turn of the page, journey with me into the unknown as I endeavour to seek that which is considered to be within the realms of the paranormal.

FOREWORD

GHOSTS have fascinated me for over forty years, so it was inevitable that the many tales and accounts of Irish ghosts would draw my attention. Although I am English, my family has strong historical links to Ireland and there is almost certainly more than one or two strands of Irish DNA floating around in my genes.

Since moving to West Wales almost eight years ago I have come to know and love the south-east of Ireland, just about visible on the clearest day from the highest Pembrokeshire hilltops. West Wales and south-east Ireland share a strong connection that predates written history and encompasses some of the key moments in our shared history, from the barrow builders to the present day.

I have enjoyed and endured the pleasures and perils of numerous trips on the Pembroke to Rosslare ferry and have had the opportunity to explore some of County Wexford's haunted locations and to seek its ghosts. So it was both an honour and a pleasure to be invited by Michael to write the foreword to *Haunted Wexford*.

Haunted Wexford visits some of the county's most famous and historical locations and presents the reader with an account of contemporary ghost investigating. Some of the techniques and methods of the modern ghost investigator, as with almost everything to do with ghosts, is open to debate and to question; ghosts are a subject that stirs the passions of believers and sceptics alike and debate is the lot of those who choose to pursue them. As Michael states, we need to encourage a shift in emphasis from seeking proof to seeking the evidence, which, over time, will lead to discovery.

From the historic landmarks of County Wexford – Enniscorthy Castle and Duncannon Fort to the comfortable modern houses of Wexford Town – we are taken behind the scenes as Michael and his team of investigators research the location, discover the history and reveal the background behind the hauntings. We join the team as they investigate and learn about the techniques and methods that are employed in the search for evidence of the paranormal. We share the many challenges that face the modern seeker of answers to the endless questions that ghosts and the paranormal pose.

Many books have been written about ghosts and ghost hunting, from straightforward gazetteers containing spooky tales of the paranormal to the 'How To' guides and heavyweight academic tomes, but Michael has written a book that is both informative and eminently readable; a book that will appeal to both the seasoned ghost hunter and those who are simply curious to learn more about the ghosts that inhabit and haunt County Wexford.

During my visits to the south-east of Ireland I have wandered through Wexford Town, Enniscorthy and New Ross and looked in countless bookstores and shops seeking out books about the ghosts and hauntings of that region. My search has mostly been in vain so it is a pleasure to discover that Michael has at last written the book I have been looking for. I hope you will enjoy reading it as much as I have.

Steve Parsons, 2014

INTRODUCTION

HERE are things in this world that we do not currently understand, or, as I write this, that we even know exist! This point, I believe, is irrefutable. Whether we are talking in terms of biology, physics or chemistry, or any field that fits into any or all of these contexts, there is not one person on this planet who would suggest that this is not the case.

That is why, in the case of any research or analysis designed to push the boundaries of human understanding, there will be debate. While this is often poorly received, it is in fact this very debate that propels any area of research forward. After all, finding answers only has value if it allows us a pathway to the next pertinent question.

What is a ghost? It would make little sense to progress any further without considering the very thing that lies at the centre of this book: ghosts. You could ask ten people this very question and get what might amount to ten different answers. Popular thinking, however, considers a ghost to be that of the soul or spirit of a deceased person. This is evidential in the

dictionary definition of a ghost: 'the non-physical part of a person believed to live on after death' (Collins English Dictionary).

However, the standard definition of a ghost – the manifestation of the soul or spirit of a deceased person by the means of a mist or a semi-transparent human form – does not account for the many thousands of cases where people have reported phantom ships, cars, carriages, or houses that no longer occupy the space in which they once stood. Clearly these things never possessed a soul or spirit and yet, on an almost daily basis, people continue to report such sightings. This also provokes the question: why do people see ghosts wearing clothes rather than being naked?

Some modern proponents of the paranormal field put forward the theory that ghosts and spirits are actually different things. If we were to attempt to get closer to an accurate definition they would suggest that a ghost is more of a residual effect, a memory of an event that, while it is experienced by the observer, has no aspect of consciousness. A spirit, on the other hand, arguably has an inherent intelligence, that being a consciousness and an awareness of its current existence, and furthermore a presence with which the observer can engage and interact.

This explains, to some degree, the paranormal, and this is what we mean by experiencing and investigating the paranormal. However, although controversy is part of this field, it is still a valid and considered field of research, interest, and pursuit, which causes as much debate as the subject matter, even amongst those who are actively involved in this area. In the microcosm of investigators and researchers, practices vary as much as the professionals involved. What are the best pieces of equipment to use? How many people should be involved in a team? Should you just use only science? Or should you only use spiritual approaches? Or should a team utilise a balanced mix of both? These, and more, I have encountered time and again in my work, and to answer them fully would require a lengthy thesis by itself, but in the interests of conciseness: it depends.

The difficulty with the scientific approach is rooted in the argument that we are nowhere near advanced enough in the equipment we use to effectively research the subject, nor are we usually in laboratory conditions to easily replicate the phenomena, so the difficulties are numerous in answering currently held assumptions about what spirits or ghosts are, what they are made up of, and what type of tools we should use to measure, and dare I say 'prove' their existence. Similarly, the argument against the spiritual approach is rooted in the idea that this is, by its very nature, subjective and as such it is the desire of the individual that brings about the respective phenomena, such as glasses moving and

tables being tipped. Alongside this is the point that we cannot use the paranormal to prove the paranormal. Therefore it depends on what the investigation team want to achieve – an experience or research?

There are a lot of very good investigative teams in this field across the world. I have had the pleasure of working with some very learned and gifted people who have advanced my skills as well as challenging my beliefs, which have had to evolve along with the evidence.

Proof is, of course, important, but beyond that I want to encourage a shift from the pressure of finding proof to that of collecting evidence, which, over time, will lead to the discovery of a more important truth, allowing for a shared journey while being open to differences in approach and experiencing this as an asset that we should learn from rather than perceive as a liability. If we could do this, we could dispose of intolerance, fear of difference and exclusivity, and move away from a mind-set and paradigm of blinkered reasons to a more inclusive outlook.

This book explores some of the locations I have visited over the years with clients and in structured investigations, either with my team, Wexford Paranormal, or as a lone investigator, as well as noted stories that have endured through the mists of time and local folklore.

Note: Footage to some of the locations contained in this book is available online at www.youtube.com/user/wexfordparanormal.

In some instances names may have been changed or omitted for reasons of privacy but this does not affect the nature or accuracy of the story.

1

WHO'S THERE?

AS a means to illustrate some of the reasoning that led me to explore the unexplained and paranormal realms of this world, I offer the following story in an attempt to demonstrate my desire to know more. Perhaps this may strike a chord of similarity that has led you to the same place. They say that charity begins at home but in the case of the following story, so does meeting a ghost …

Born in February 1971, I grew up in Wexford Town in the south-east corner of Ireland. Although now a more vibrant

Wexford Town is steeped in stories of the unexplained.

country, growing up in the Ireland of the 1970s and '80s was a very different picture. Unemployment was high and work was scarce. For the ordinary man on the street income was low and disposable income was so rare that the very term 'disposable income' enjoyed the status of being almost nonexistent.

My father worked in a factory, as did many of the men in the town, his job being to spray-paint cars in a production facility, while my mom stayed at home to look after me and, over time, my two younger sisters.

Looking back, this was a simpler time in many ways. My sister and I would wait each evening for our dad to return from work, knowing that hidden in his blazer pocket there would be a packet of chewy sweets for both of us. This was something

he did the evening of each working day without fail. Stopping at the local shop on the way home, this exercise would cost him the princely sum of tuppence, but to us the experience was priceless!

Dad's blazer, the one he always wore to work, was a deep burgundy red colour with paint stains that often matched the colours on his nose from the cars he had been painting that day.

Our house was exactly the same as the other houses in the estate, with the exception of the personal touches placed on them by the families as they moved in. Windows painted a different colour or lawns dressed in different ways were the only things that set one house apart from the other.

This particular supernatural experience centred on a bucket of coal and that of my

Turning around, I saw the ghostly figure of a woman standing in the gateway. (Artist's impression)

impending Confirmation ceremony. The night before my Confirmation my mother asked me to go outside and bring in a bucket of coal to keep the fire going. It was March and the weather was still cold. So it was that I found myself digging feverishly at the coal heap in an attempt to fill the bucket quickly and get back inside.

'Michael!' I heard my name called. Frustrated at having the focus of my endeavours interrupted, I dropped the shovel and headed inside.

'What do you want?' I asked my mother, thinking she had called me from inside the house.

'I didn't call you,' she said in quick response.

Returning outside to the shovel once again, I had barely recommenced when again I heard 'Michael!' This time, suspecting that someone was playing tricks, I walked through the back gate of our end-of-terrace house, turned the corner and looked over the boundary wall into the neighbour's garden in the hope of finding one of my friends hiding there shaking with laughter … there was no one to be seen.

It was dark outside and this, along with the cold weather, was enough reason for me to want to get myself back inside as soon as was humanly possible. I sought to conclude my digging when for a third time I heard 'Michael!'

I wheeled around quickly, hoping to catch whoever it was that was having such fun at my expense. What I saw instead was an old woman standing in the gateway through which I had just returned, ambient light from the street shining from behind, silhouetting her form in the open gateway.

Where this story moves away from what we might be inclined to consider the mundane or ordinary is the fact that, although this woman stood in silhouette, I found that I could also see through her form as though it were semi-transparent; I could see details from the street that would otherwise be masked were this person a solid form.

I was the only great-grandchild born before my great-grandmother on my mother's side passed away. Could this have been her checking in given, the milestone occasion taking place the next day? Although some forty years have since passed, she is welcome to stop by anytime.

2

ENNISCORTHY CASTLE

THERE is no landmark in County Wexford more instantly recognisable or more readily called to mind than that of Enniscorthy Castle. A prominent landmark overlooking the river Slaney, nestled in the shadow of Vinegar Hill, Enniscorthy Castle has stood as silent witness to over 800 years of significant Irish social history.

First records point to a building being established on this site as early as 1190, when Phillip de Prendergast, having married a woman by the name of Maud de Quency, resided at the castle until the time of his death in the year 1229.

We must, however, jump forward almost 400 years to the year 1585, when ownership of the castle passed by royal appointment to one Henry Wallop who, it is reported, brought significant wealth to the town of Enniscorthy through the exploitation of much of the woodland and forestry in the area and, using some of the finances gained from this, he restored the castle into the structure that we recognise and still see today.

In 1649 the castle came to the attention of Oliver Cromwell, who laid siege to it. On this occasion it was only the early surrender of those defending the fortification that ensured it remained intact and did not fall foul to the ferocity with which Cromwell and his forces carried out their actions.

One of the most significant events in Wexford's history, ingrained in the fabric of any Wexfordian, is the failed rebellion of 1798, culminating in the Battle of Vinegar Hill in June of that year, with the hill itself being clearly visible from the castle. One can only attempt to imagine the treatment meted out on those who were captured during this turbulent time. In fact, history has reported that over a very short six-week period as many as 20,000 people, the majority of them women and children, lost their lives.

During this time the castle acted as a prison when the ground floor and lower ground dungeon or oubliette (as it is referred to in Hore's *History of Wexford*) were the principal locations used to incarcerate those taken as prisoners.

Punishments such as pitch capping and half-hangings were reported to be numbered among some of the favoured methods of torture inflicted on suspected rebels at the castle. Pitch capping involved pouring hot pitch on the head of a victim, forming a 'cap' on the head. Once the pitch had cooled the cap would then be torn off, bringing with it both the hair and in most cases many layers of skin as well. The infections that would have resulted from such torture often led to the ultimate demise of the prisoner.

Some 100 years after the rising the castle was leased to the Roche family, becoming their family home until 1951. However, the Roche family were temporarily ousted from their home in 1916 by the Irish Volunteers, and again in 1922, during which time the castle was commandeered by the Free State Army.

Eleven years after the Roche family left the castle it opened to the public as a county museum, a function it retained until it finally closed its doors in 2006.

The following five years saw the castle left to itself, its history and even perhaps its ghosts, until it opened its doors once again to the public in 2011 refreshed, renewed and this time adapting the central role of telling the story of Enniscorthy's evolution, this time through the very eyes of the castle itself.

In March 2011 my phone rang. I answered it to the enthusiastic voice of a woman. 'Hi, my name is Jacqui and I am the Manager of Enniscorthy Castle.' Immediately my interest was piqued. Jacqui went on to say:

I saw an article about your team in the paper and I was interested to know if you might consider coming along and checking out the castle. We think we might have a ghost. At the very least, there seems to be something strange going on!

Needless to say any opportunity to investigate claims of possible paranormal activity is something that we greet with both interest and enthusiasm, but when the call relates to a location as significant in the context of Wexford history as that of Enniscorthy Castle and is also a location that has never before been investigated, then the prospect of venturing into uncharted territory is even more exciting.

You could well suggest that the prospect of spending long hours of darkness in an 800-year-old castle is borderline madness, and indeed you may well be right, but it is what we do.

In an attempt to gather as much information as I could with regard to the nature and extent of the supposed activity, I asked Jacqui what had been happening.

Where do I begin? First I am not even sure what I think about all of this myself! That said, however, only this week we had a mother and daughter visiting at the castle and during their visit they had ascended the stairway at the front of the castle.

This stairway is a spiral design made up of granite stone steps and is an original feature of the castle.

Jacqui continued with her story.

While the other members of staff present on this occasion, myself included, were down in the reception area, located on the ground floor and to the front of the castle, the mother in question returned to us and asked with some slight annoyance as to who had called out to her daughter by name? We were quick to point out that it could not have been any of us as we did not know her daughter's name as some visitors forget to sign the visitor's book and for the most part those that do only do so once they have completed their visit and are just about to leave. What we did not point out to her, however, was the fact that at this particular time we were the only other people in the castle, discretion being the better option so as not to alarm our visitor.

This story turned out to be just the tip of the iceberg. Jacqui went on to disclose how there were already numerous reports by different people, made at different times and on different days none of whom apparently knew each other. These particular reports all consisted of claims of a dark, shadow-like figure being seen and all of the reports identified the very same point on the stairs, just where the spiral staircase passes the door that enters into the room on the second floor containing artefacts from the 1916 Rising (this particular location would result in some very fascinating events during a later investigation for a programme called *Paranormal Journeys,* more on this later), before passing into the Eileen Grey room which displays replica examples of the works by the famous Wexford designer.

Jacqui also mentioned claims of footsteps being heard on the floorboards of the sitting room situated on the first floor, reports of children's voices being heard and a report by one of the male members of staff who, opening up one morning, entered the castle to hear voices in the back room having a full-blown conversation. This resulted in him remaining in the front porch of the entrance – for fear perhaps of what he might discover were he to venture any further – until the arrival of another member of staff.

Jacqui also recounted one personal experience she herself had.

> I was coming down the back stairs, something I do numerous times each day, but as I approached the bottom of the stairs on this occasion I felt like I was pushed from behind. I know tripping on a step is something easily done and in truth I have had such experiences in the past, at least enough times to know that this felt different.

At this point no mention of the oubliette or dungeon that passes beneath the ground floor level had been made.

A follow-up visit was made to the castle, where I met with Jacqui and took a walk with her, visiting each location and revisiting the stories she had shared with me during our previous telephone conversation.

A date for the investigation was subsequently fixed for a night during the following two weeks. As circumstance would have it, Colette Brown, a journalist at the time with a local paper, was doing a follow-up feature on Wexford Paranormal and so it was that on this occasion both Collette and a press photographer joined us in the castle on the night.

Our investigation started at a low point, quite literally, as we made our

Enniscorthy Castle. (© M. Benson)

way down to the back chamber of the oubliette. As one leaves the comfort of the entrance space to venture down into the oubliette it becomes an exercise in negotiating a series of narrow steps, before entering a small front chamber with a low ceiling that is hewn from the very rock on top of which the castle is built. From here we passed through a narrow central arch into the circular back chamber in which we would make our first attempt to connect with anything, be it spirit, presence or entity that may reside in this space.

A carving in the back wall depicting the figure of a soldier caught my eye in the light of my torch. Noticing that it had caught my attention, Jacqui pointed out that this was in fact that of a halberdier and current enquiry seeks to ascertain if it originates from the sixteenth century or, as popular thinking suggests, it relates to the rebellion of 1798.

We took up our positions seated on the floor – the group consisted of a number of the team along with the castle manager, press journalist and photographer – and allowed a short time for the space to settle before we started to call out.

The darkness that erupted once I had switched off my torch was all encompassing, an absolute darkness that offered little forgiveness even after pupils had dilated in response to the lack of any ambient light.

As we progressed with our enquiry responses started to come in a manner such as knocks and thuds that, as well as being heard in the confinement of our current location, could also be 'felt' by way of a vibration of sorts in the very fabric of the stone walls that surrounded us.

At this point I should mention some of the equipment that we use on such investigations. Too numerous to discuss in any great detail, these include such devices as EMF (electromagnetic field) measuring devices as well as audio and night-vision video equipment. Also on the floor was a small black box resembling a portable radio, which is, in fact, what it was before adaptations had turned it into a device known in the paranormal community as a Frank's Box. It is called this after its creator, Frank Sumpton, and no piece of equipment divides the paranormal community as much as this. Some teams like to use it as part of their investigation process while others completely dismiss it out of hand. The theory is that as a detuned AM radio, it constantly scans the frequency band and a presence or spirit can use the white noise and harmonics to allow real-time communication with anyone using it. In the interests of maintaining a balance of argument, some people would argue, however, that it is nothing more than random noise and that we as humans add meaning to what we hear, a sort of audible pareidolia if you will, when the human brain seeks to make form out of randomness. What I will add at this point based on my own personal experience is that reason and experience do not always follow parallel paths. From a perspective of reason I can accept that this device is only a construction of electrical components; however, I have had far too many experiences of using it to suggest it is nothing more. While explaining its purpose and use to those joining us on the night, I called out and asked that, if there was anyone with us, would they tell us their name please?

Following this everyone present heard the name 'Jim' being relayed back through the device – those experiencing it for the first time reacting with some surprise. I explained that when we get one word responses we ask the question again on more than one occasion, to ensure a consistency of response. To illustrate this to those gathered in the dungeon I again asked, 'Can you do that again? Can you tell us your name please?' For a second time the name 'Jim' came back to us through the Frank's Box.

Because we were under the additional scrutiny of the local press I wanted to reinforce the point, and so I asked the question one more time just for good measure. 'I'm sorry, can I ask you to do that one more time. Can you tell me your name please?' This time we got an answer and with it a very definite expression of sentiment when back came the reply, 'MY NAME IS JIM,' as if to suggest with slight annoyance, how many more times are you going to ask me? So it was that we encountered Jim for the first time!

In later visits to the castle I, along with the rest of the team in Wexford Paranormal, have spent many hours there, most of which were cloaked in the enveloping darkness of the castle environs. During these visits 'Jim' continued to communicate with us and over

The dungeons of Enniscorthy Castle. (© M. Benson)

time has shared with us his wife's name, his son's name and indeed his surname. We shared this information with Jacqui, the castle manager, who later informed us that she had, in fact, located Jim and his family in the 1901 census! We now know where he lived in Enniscorthy, what age he was in that year, the age of his wife and son and even the name of an additional person who was staying with the family on the night that the census was completed. Further research by our Team Historical Research member revealed that the family were not in Enniscorthy ten years later, when the 1911 census was completed, but we do know that they had returned to Enniscorthy by 1914, as Jim appears on the Register of Electors list for an election taking place that year.

While at the castle, recording a show for broadcast over Halloween with Tony Scott and the South East Radio Crew, a member of their crew spent time alone in one of the turret rooms on the roof of the castle. Subsequent review of the footage revealed that a disembodied voice had been captured responding to a question during the session.

Since our discovery of Jim in Enniscorthy Castle there have been visits by a number of other paranormal investigation teams, all of whom have reported unexplained activity during their visits there.

Following a lecture at the castle by Barry Fitzgerald, well known for his work with Ghost Hunters International, I was showing members of the Kilkenny Investigative Paranormal Society (KIPS)

The turret on the roof of the castle, where a disembodied voice has been heard on two separate occasions. (© M. Benson)

around the castle. We were standing in the drawing room on the first floor discussing what had been reported at the castle. While the floor in this room is timber, there is a flagstone section that surrounds the fireplace that is some 5ft by 8ft in size. We happened to all be standing on this section of flagstone when, not 2ft away from us, a very loud bang was heard on the wooden floor, almost as if someone had jumped in the air and then landed resolutely back on the floor with both feet! There was of course that momentary silent as each person looked around to ensure that everyone had heard the same thing. It was about 10.30 p.m., all the lights were on, no one else was in the castle and we all had heard the same thing!

As the crew from KIPS were leaving the castle that night, we could hear voices coming from the floor above. We approached the bottom of the stone staircase to see if we could hear it more clearly as the conversation continued. I called out and asked, 'Jim, we are about to leave but the guys are planning to come back. Did you want to say goodbye?' Immediately there came from the first floor a loud bang, which we acknowledged as his way of saying goodbye, and we left the building to its own devices.

During filming for a programme titled *Paranormal Journeys*, Mike Hirons, founder and Lead Investigator with Ulster Paranormal, was visiting locations around Ireland, one in each province, and at each location he also invited a guest investigator along. I had the pleasure of joining him on the Leinster shoot to be filmed at Enniscorthy Castle.

During the course of the investigation we were filming on the first floor when we get a call from Base Station … 'Michael, does your geophone flash?' Because of the reports of activity regarding this shadow figure, we had set up a motion sensor and a geophone at the location where the shadow figure has been reported to be seen. The motion sensor was placed in the window and if anything seen or unseen passed it the light would come on. The geophone was placed on a step below the window and, designed to activate in response to vibration, it would respond should anything move in the general area. On this occasion we had the sensitivity set so that only movement from two steps above or below would cause a response and on this particular stone staircase there was very little chance that vibration would travel any distance at all. We then placed a night vision CCTV camera on a ledge above the location, to ensure we had it all on camera.

'It does flash,' I responded on the walkie-talkie, 'but we are on the first floor, we will go and check it out.' Mike, Wendy (who was a Para Analyst on the show), John the cameraman and I headed up to the location. Arriving there we found the motion sensor was also on! Later review of the CCTV footage would reveal that this had in fact happened a full fifteen seconds before we had arrived at the location.

Vinegar Hill seen from the roof of Enniscorthy Castle. (© M. Benson)

The point on the stairwell where visitors report seeing a shadow figure. (© M. Benson)

Eager to explore this further, Mike invited whoever was there 'to light the light on the window'. In response to this request the motion sensor light came on, followed by flashing of the geophone, suggesting that someone had just passed the motion sensor and continued up the stairs, causing the flashing on the geophone. This 'presence' was then invited to make the geophone flash and, with almost immediate response, the geophone did indeed flash. This was followed by the light coming on at the sensor in the window, suggesting that whatever was there had returned down the stairs. In each case we could see nobody other than ourselves at the location and this interactive communication continued for a period of some forty minutes.

Shortly after this, two of the crew entered one of the turret rooms while the rest of us took a well-earned break back at base. Both of them returned in a very excited manner carrying with then an old dictaphone that they had been using to attempt to capture some EVP (Electronic Voice Phenomena). 'Listen to what we just caught,' both of them said excitedly. When the tape was played back we could hear both of them discussing the location followed by a dog barking and a lady's voice saying 'Help me!' Relative to the proximity of the voices of the crew, the bark and the female voice sounded as if they had come from right beside the microphone!

Another story of this location comes from the guys in Causeway Paranormal, who conducted an overnight investigation at the castle in late 2011. During the course of the investigation Wendy Colson, the founder of the team, reported the following experiences:

While in the castle we could clearly hear voices. We followed the voices in the direction from which we thought they were coming and this led us to a small corridor that had an old wooden door that exited out into the side entrance of the castle.

There were three of us there, Rob, Kelly Anne and myself. We were looking out through one of the windows in an attempt to discover if anyone had come down the side entrance of the castle and were in actual fact having a conversation outside. What we discovered was an empty space and as we were about to move from this location, a fire extinguisher – which was on a heavy chrome stand some 4 or 5ft to our left – was knocked over, stand and all! We have no explanation for this and in fact we even tried to replicate this only to find that significant force would be required to cause it to topple over. We have no explanation for it!

When I was in the sitting room on the first floor the armchair next to the fireplace which I was standing some 2ft behind moved forward on its own. It was an amazing experience in an amazing place!

Recently two people visiting from Canada were being shown around the castle after hours as they were friends with one of the members of the Wexford Paranormal team. During this visit they spent some time in the dark on the first floor of the castle and were trying some of the various pieces of investigative equipment. Over the course of this session the sound of footsteps could be heard coming from the floor above, causing one of our guests to ask, 'Do you want us to go upstairs?' We jokingly made the observation that he probably hadn't had that kind of invitation in quite some time! She then continued, 'Would you like to go upstairs with me Jim? Would you like to go to the bedroom?' As our guest put the headphones back over her ears to listen, the answer that followed surprised us all. We could all clearly hear coming from the device the answer, 'If you want to go to bed, why don't you go to bed by yourself?' Jim, if indeed that was who we were speaking to, is clearly a man of old world morals.

People continue to visit and enjoy Enniscorthy Castle on a daily basis and reports continue to surface regarding unexplained and possible paranormal activity at the castle.

3

LOFTUS HALL

STORIES become tales, tales become fables and fables, over time, become legends. This surely has to be the case where Loftus Hall is concerned. The mists of time hide any absolute truths that may lie behind the legends that we have come to know.

Much has been written over the centuries and indeed much of that will be recounted here, but, alongside these stories, tales, legends (call them what you will), I will also share with you the story of the night spent at Loftus Hall with my team, exploring the history of Loftus Hall through the eyes of contemporary paranormal enthusiasts and paranormal investigators.

Situated on an isolated peninsula, Loftus Hall holds a lonely vigil over the Waterford estuary, clearly a calculated decision in the defensive positioning of the building itself. Flat barren land makes the Hall visible from some distance in all directions and alongside the enigma that is the Hall stands one lonely, wind-beaten tree.

Often referred to as the most haunted place in Ireland, Loftus Hall would not seem out of place in a Brontë novel, with the figures of Heathcliff and Catherine blending seamlessly into the vista that the current Loftus Hall creates.

In the year 1350 the Black Death held Ireland in its grip and it is against this turbulent backdrop that the first incarnation of the Hall is referenced. Research would suggest that this particular building was built mainly of red brick with four towers, one at each corner of the structure that offered defensive fortification of the courtyard that the walls surrounded. The remains of one of the towers can still be found, to one side of the location where the present Hall stands, in what is known locally as the ring field.

In one book written around the turn of the last century, credit for the building of this stronghold is given to Raymond, who was one of Strongbow's followers. It remained in the possession of his descendants until it was forfeited in 1641 during the rebellion of that year referenced through history as the Irish Confederate Wars.

In the following year (1642) a ship was taken from Duncannon by one Captain Ashton (also recorded as Aston) whose plan it was to take the Hall, given its strategic position. A determined and enthusiastic man, it would appear, however, that his enthusiasm far outweighed his skill and experience as a military strategist. Captain Ashton had been instructed by Lord Esmonde, who at that time was Commander of Duncannon Fort, to approach by sea and that should the first attack of Ordnance not cause the Hall to yield, that he should keep his men together and return to the fort at Duncannon.

In order to do this Ashton took with him some ninety men and two small cannon with which he planned to breech the Hall.

At this time Alexander Redmond was in possession of the Hall and although he was some sixty-eight years of age, it was he, along with a small number of people including his two sons Robert and Michael, who managed to ensure Captain Ashton would be unsuccessful in his endeavours, managing to hold fast in the Hall until the noise from the skirmish led to other Confederate troops in the area arriving to attack the invaders. In fact, Captain Ashton himself, along with a number of the crew, was killed during the attack while others were taken prisoner with some thirty more managing to escape and return to Duncannon Fort. Records of the time indicate that having initially been given quarter, Captain Ashton was subsequently killed and his head taken to Wexford. Of those who were captured, reports would suggest that some seven were hanged the next day while that those remaining were taken to New Ross only to suffer the same fate.

Loftus Hall. (© M. Benson)

Some seven years later Alexander, who by now had reached his seventy-fifth year, found himself having to defend the Hall from a number of attacks by Cromwell's forces. Ultimately Alexander surrendered the Hall to Cromwell and in return was granted favourable conditions and permission to continue living there until his death some two years later.

So it was that in 1650 the Hall passed into the hands of the Loftus family. An Act of Settlement cemented the change of ownership to the Loftus family and this event took place on 30 September 1666.

Much had been made of the significance of the last three digits of that year and their association with the legend that endures regarding the mysterious visitor to the Hall and the events that were said to unfold. Some go so far as to suggest that this is by no means mere coincidence but instead another clue that points to the validity of the legend.

In 1672 the events pertaining to the legend of Loftus Hall began to unfold.

Charles Tottenham lived at the Hall at this time along with his two daughters, Elizabeth and Anne. Both daughters were from his first marriage but by then he had married for a second time. Legend has it that Charles was a man with little tendency to humour and the relationship between Anne and her stepmother was one of intolerance at best.

One narrator when recounting this story in a publication from the turn of the last century describes the Hall thus: 'It was an old rambling mansion, with no pretence to beauty: passages that led nowhere, large dreary rooms, small closets, various unnecessary nooks and corners, panelled or wainscoted walls and a tapestry chamber.'

One very wet and stormy night the family were startled by a knock to the door. One of the servants returned from answering the door and informed Charles that there was a young gentleman who had arrived on horseback having lost his way and, with his horse now lame, he was requesting a kindness of the family by way of board and lodging. He had been guided there by the light of the house, which had been the only light he had seen since becoming lost. Other variations to the tale suggest he had made his way there following a shipwreck in the area.

Having been granted the shelter he was seeking, this stranger proved himself to be a most agreeable guest and was reported to be a very well finished gentleman indeed. Anne, seeing few people other than her father and stepmother (even her sister Elizabeth had married and moved from the Hall), developed a strong attraction to the young man, one which he willingly reciprocated and upon his leaving she was so succumbed by grief that she lost all reason and became a maniac. The result was that Anne was confined to the Tapestry Room until the time of her death.

Rather than have the family status and position brought into disrepute by association with that of a maniac daughter, a story was constructed that was to endure through the centuries.

The story goes that the agreeable nature of their guest was such that he was invited to remain on for a while and now that there were four of them there each evening (Charles, his wife, Anne and the aforementioned stranger) a card game was proposed. Charles and his wife were partnered for this game and Anne was partnered with the visiting stranger. Hand after hand and game after game, success ensued for Anne and her partner with Charles and his wife enjoying no success at all. Such was Anne's excitement that during one game her ring inadvertently dropped from her hand onto the floor. Bending down quickly to retrieve the ring, Anne had the unfortunate experience of noticing that her partner in this game had a cloven foot and must therefore have been the devil. The scream that ensued at once alerted the stranger to the fact that his true identity had been discovered, upon which he vanished through the roof in a flash of light and to a thunderous sound, leaving behind the unmistakable smell of brimstone in the room.

The story goes that Anne never recovered from the shock and it is for this reason that she was confined to the Tapestry Room until her death some three years later. During this time she was reported to have refused food and drink and as a result of maintaining the same posture seated in this room for so long, it proved impossible to alter this position even after her death, resulting in a special shaped coffin having to be made to accommodate Anne's body.

It is suggested that subsequent visits were made to the Hall by the devil and he continued to disturb those living there.

Following Anne's death in 1775, it is suggested that her ghost was seen many times at the Hall and such was the level of noises and apparitions that, even though the family in residence were not of a Catholic persuasion, the services of one Fr Thomas Broaders were brought to bear and, employing all of the exorcism techniques of the Catholic Church, he succeeded in banishing, or at least confining, the activities of this ghost to one room, known to be the Tapestry Room.

There are also suggestions that one Revd George Reid had occasion to visit the Hall to attend a function and, given the lateness of his arrival and the number of others staying there that night, he found that he was assigned the Tapestry Room as his sleeping quarters. Thinking little of the stories of the Hall, he retired to bed happily enough. But he had scarcely lay beneath the blankets when something unseen launched itself upon his bed, growling like a deranged animal. Managing to light the room by means of either a match or candle, he discovered after a thorough search that the room was empty and that the door was still locked from the inside, as he had left it upon retiring for the night.

Many years later, another visitor, in fact the son of Revd Reid and also called George, came to the Hall and also stayed in the Tapestry Room. One night he saw a lady dressed in brocaded silk enter the room through the door and advance through the room to a closet, whereupon she disappeared. This happened again the following night and this time, with the resolve to catch whoever it was that was having fun at his expense, the guest lunged forward and attempted to grab this nocturnal visitor, only for his arms to pass right through the apparition, grabbing instead one of the bedposts close by.

In 1870, history tells us that the Hall was razed to the ground and the building that we see today took up residence in its stead, having been constructed on the foundations of the original Redmond Hall. Thomas P. Walsh, writing about the history of Loftus Hall in the *Old Wexford Society Journal* (Walsh, 1971), states that:

Redmond's Hall is gone and has been replaced by the modern Loftus Hall … The story occurred, not in the present Hall, but in the renovated Redmond's Hall, already mentioned, and the affair happened between 1731 and 1775 … Tradition has it that until the Hall was demolished in 1870, the hole in the ceiling, through which the cloven-footed gentleman vanished, resisted all attempts at repair, and remained a gaping monument to his memory. Between 1870 and 1871 the old Hall was levelled to the ground by the fourth Marquis of Ely, and the present Loftus Hall was built on the same site.

In the years that followed, the hall was occupied by two orders of nuns before being bought in the 1980s and used as a hotel until it closed in the late 1990s. It has lain destitute ever since.

On 18 February 2011, I and my team of investigators from Wexford Paranormal arrived at the Hall under a cloak of rain coupled with that of a harassing sea mist.

Loftus Hall, once splendid in its lavish beauty, is now nothing more than a sinister shadow of its former self. This location had been on our radar for some considerable time, so to have the invitation to investigate this most noted and allegedly haunted of locations excited us greatly.

All of the usual protocols were observed as we first conducted a health and safety review of the location in order to cordon off areas that were unsafe for either passage or entry, as the ravages of time and neglect has laid waste to many of its floors without consideration or mercy. The grand staircase too was beginning to take leave of its original structure and shape, as piece by piece sections of inlaid wood, with the assistance of prevailing dampness and gravity, sought to make good their escape from the locations intended for them by their original craftsmen.

Period furniture stood in many of the rooms with fine china contained therein, ready to be used again at a moment's notice were it not for the settled layers of dust that now lined each piece. In the many bedrooms, clothes continue to hang in their wardrobes with the exception of occasional pieces that had been removed and strewn about by previous uninvited visitors and vandals. Down one of the long halls on the ground floor, lying against one of the walls, was a large crucifix that one can only assume was a testament to the time when Loftus Hall was occupied by an order of nuns. Another indicator of their time spent here was found in one of the small side rooms which, judging by the numerous arched brick receptacles, must have started life as a wine storage unit. For now though it seemed their job was to house framed Stations of the Cross that would have once hung in the chapel.

First impressions would almost suggest sudden, overnight abandonment of the Hall, the reason for which could only at best be speculated upon but needless to say did little to relax the minds of the new and uninitiated members of the team.

So with CCTV camera locations established, the equipment was set up and at 10.30 p.m. the team split into two to begin the night's journey into the unknown.

Concerned with not losing their way in the dark, the first team of five made their way cautiously towards the function room. Upon entering one of the long halls, they were just about to call out when they heard a banging noise from behind. Responding to this, Veronica, one of the members of this team, called out, 'Is there anyone here with us?' Looking down the hall, Veronica was startled into saying, 'Holy s★★t!', prompting another member of the group to quickly ask what she had seen. 'Oh my God, I thought I saw … someone walked … did someone just walk down there?' said Veronica. 'That has freaked me! I'm after getting a big fright.'

Veronica thought she had seen Michael Carroll, who is the tech specialist with the team. At 6 feet 4 inches tall Michael does indeed cast an imposing presence; the only problem with Veronica's assumption was that Michael, along with the other half of the team, was at another location at the opposite end of the building. Veronica's team were therefore alone and left with their first unexplained experience of the night.

The group invited whatever had shown itself to do so again, but without success. Asking if it wanted them to leave the area resulted in an immediate response on the EMF meter, causing the lights to go all the way to red. While perhaps only coincidental, this had not happened before asking the question and did not happen again during this stage of the investigation. This device measures electromagnetic fields and with a strict team policy of not having mobile phones on location we know that whatever had caused this, it was not the signal of a mobile phone.

Hollie, another team member, later recalled:

The thing I really remember was going down the hallway where we got that response from the EMF when we asked if it wanted us to leave. The further we went down the hallway the more dark it seemed to get and the more uneasy I felt. It was like we were going into its territory. We tried to keep going but it was almost like a huge energetic barrier stopping us!

Team two were on the first floor later into the investigation, while Michael Carroll and I were manning the CCTV monitors back at base station. Breda, one of the members of team two, was sitting on a bed on the first floor and felt as if something had sat on the bed behind her. Paul, who was also there, radioed down to us to enquire if we could see anything on the cameras. While there were observable movement and shadows such things could be accounted for by way of dust and movement of light as a result of the movement of video cameras and the infrared light that they use to record in the darkness. While it can be argued that such an experience is personal and subjective, it is an experience none the less and, taken in context with the story of growling entities leaping on beds, it makes the correlation somewhat more interesting!

We had been led to understand that one of the nuns who resided at the Hall had passed away from a heart attack on the back stairs, just at the turn of the staircase (a story we could not corroborate afterwards). Taking this on board, we decided to place both audible motion sensors and a geophone to measure vibration that may be caused by the footfall of an unseen observer on the middle of this stairs and to then lock off a CCTV camera to capture anything that may occur. At a point in the night when none of the teams were in the area the geophone began to flash with no apparent explanation.

Around this time both teams began to report observing lights underneath the doorways in the halls. Both teams reported that these lights were blue in colour.

While conducting an EVP session, one of the teams reported how one of the large wardrobes seemed to bang, as if lifted from the floor slightly and allowed to fall back to the ground. Speaking about it afterwards, Hollie said, 'The wardrobe just lifted and smacked down! It was so quick. There was an almighty bang and no one was anywhere near it!'

On his way back to the base station Robbie, another member of the team, was taking general photographs. While we shoot a lot of photos in infrared we also take them in a conventional manner, using a standard flash camera. As he approached the turning point of the ornate front stairs, looking down he could see the central door behind which other members of the team were sitting at the table that contained the CCTV monitoring system. In fact, this particular door at one time would have had two upright glass panels in the top half, which were now missing, and the cables from our CCTV cameras were now running through the space where the glass had been and from there followed their individual route to the camera to which they were now attached.

'I didn't notice anything at the time,' said Robbie. 'It wasn't until later when we were reviewing the various pieces of footage that I noticed the photograph.' What was discovered in this one particular picture was that where the glass once was there appeared to be what could only be described as 'flames' coming through these panels, bright orange flames that seemed to be sweeping to the right, almost as if caught in some significant draught. Except there was no draught!

We were careful to check to ensure that what we were looking at was not contamination or flair being caused by any other light source such as the candescent bulbs in the ceiling, but taking into account the height of the ceilings in the downstairs rooms this could not have been the case. So the question remains, had we captured an image that in some way had allowed us a momentary insight into some residual image of a past event? While we can never definitively say that this was some form of paranormal occurrence, what we can certainly say is that it remains a significantly unexplained event!

Further investigation later that night using ITC (Instrumental Trans Communication) back at the function room (just beyond where the shadow figure had been seen earlier) suggested that whoever the team were communicating with appeared to have a dislike for the lady members, this being confirmed by means of choice language that will not be repeated here! Following a line of enquiry in relation to this, the investigators were prompted to ask, 'Are we all in danger?' to which they had a clear response 'Yes'! Following enquiry as to the name of our unseen visitor he indicated that his name was Seth and, when asked to repeat this again for confirmation, the name Seth was again heard for a second time. Then, to everyone's surprise, the word Satan was clearly heard from the device! If whoever it was that was communicating with us knew the legend of Loftus Hall, then they were doing their best to give us the whole show, our money's worth if you will, of that I am certain.

'Flames' in the door at Loftus Hall. (© M. Benson)

So did we meet the ghost of Anne Tottenham? I don't believe we did and we most definitely did not meet the Prince of Darkness himself, but I guess that mysteries only remain mysteries for as long as answers are not found and for the foreseeable future the legend will prevail.

While it is not the most active allegedly haunted location we have spent the night in, all of us there on the night left the location with memories that will last us a lifetime.

The Hall has passed once again into the hands of a new owner and for now at least the future of Loftus Hall and even more so the evolution of its legend has been safeguarded for coming generations.

4

THE BALLYMURN CASE

HE a aspect of paranormal investigation that interests my team and I the most is that of private cases. Opportunities to investigate in peoples' homes with the prospect of making a difference to the people who live there and who, on an almost daily basis, are having to live with the reality that something unexplained is going on in their house, is the very essence of what we are about.

There is invariably an underlying sense of fear attached to these experiences and, whether real or imagined by the person or persons involved, this results in them contacting investigators like us. For most paranormal investigation teams this is most likely the number one reason why they have set themselves up and why they do what they do.

Even in cases where there ultimately ends up being a rational explanation for the occurrences taking place, the feeling of fear or dread is always very real for the person involved. If by the time we have finished we are able to leave the client

with a significantly reduced level of fear, then we have served them well.

The biggest difficulty with private cases, however, is just that – they are private. Very often, with the exception of the family involved and any other individuals may who have shared in an experience from these locations, no one outside of the family and the members in the investigating team get to hear about the experiences.

Often, when we are contacted about a potential case, the person will most likely say, 'You will probably think I am mad but ...' or 'I can't believe I am making this call; this kind of thing just doesn't happen but ...'. I find that I have to be quick to address these issues and very often the caller is surprised to hear how often we are contacted about reports of possible paranormal activity. Sometimes even this revelation begins the process of offering some comfort to the client.

The following story is of one such private case, with the exception that in this instance the client was happy to share their story in a public capacity, motivated by the idea that if in sharing their story it encourages one other person experiencing the unexplained to pick up the phone and make a call or, if it means that it allows just one other person to realise they are not losing their mind in thinking that they are experiencing such activity, then the purpose for doing so will have been achieved.

This story started like so many others, with a phone call, and I soon found myself travelling to the leafy village of Ballymurn just beyond Olygate to meet with the client for a follow up discussion and to visit the house where the phenomena were taking place. Situated right between Wexford Town and Enniscorthy, the local church, school, shop and pub were passed in very quick succession and as I approached the house I recall thinking that one could be forgiven for assuming that nothing ever happens in Ballymurn.

When I met Yvonne Conway it was obvious from the start that here was a person with clearly defined parameters: what mattered, what didn't, what was important, what wasn't, what was accepted as normal and what didn't quite fit this model – having had some very recent experiences concerning the latter. Yvonne was clearly a person with a firm grasp on how the world works and, along with her husband, has turned that social savvy into a very successful business in up-skilling and people training services. Recent experiences, however, had taken her out of her comfort zone.

With the formalities of introduction and an explanation of how we work out of the way, we got down to talking about what had been experienced thus far.

'We were having a movie and popcorn night and we were all sitting here very relaxed,' Yvonne said.

What we heard next was a tap, tap, tap, tap along the floor to the right of me, in the direction of the windows and I thought it was my daughter Sarah Jane messing. The noise for the entire world sounded like that of a popcorn seed being thrown across our wooden floor.

Yvonne then reported that they heard the exact same sound some five minutes later. Yvonne continued:

On another occasion I was down in my bedroom, alone in the house. From the bedroom I could hear a clapping or a tapping noise. First I thought it could be coming from my neighbours. I didn't know what was going on so I stepped out into my hallway and I realised it was coming from another room so I went back in [to the bedroom], unplugged my mobile, got it onto record and walked back down to the room. The cat was sitting in the hall outside the door of the room looking in, he wasn't going in and as I got closer the noise got louder. I walked into the room and on the TV there was a white line going across and a white line going down and it was like a hammer just beating.

Yvonne had mentioned to me when we had first spoken on the phone about an incident with the electric piano, and I asked her to tell me some more about this particular occurrence.

Yes, that was really weird. I am glad there was someone there with me. I think if I had been on my own I wouldn't be too willing to tell the story. We were in my kitchen, my daughter and I, and we were looking up stuff on the internet through the laptop and my daughter just said, 'Mom, do you hear that?'

The two of us just listened and it was the piano and it was playing a low tune, not even a tune, just random keys.

Wondering if it might have been possible that the cat could have climbed up on to the keys, I enquired to that effect. Yvonne said that this was not the case and that the electric piano on this occasion was in actual fact switched off at the wall and there was no power going to it, so it could not have even been switched on!

To add more substance to this particular claim, if in fact more substance was needed, Yvonne continued:

And then there's my son, I only discovered this recently. We were talking about the piano and he said, 'Yeah Mom, I heard that too!'

I asked him when did he hear it and where were we? He said that we were all in bed asleep and that he was awake and he heard the piano!

Sarah Jane, Yvonne's daughter, had her experiences to share. She reported that on one occasion:

I was lying on the couch and upon looking up 'it' was at the bottom of the couch, and it was the figure of a man – Just over there [she pointed in the direction of the fireplace] and he

was a really, really tall man. Well over six feet. He had dark hair, dark clothes, it looked like dark jeans. I remember not being scared at the time then he looked at me and said, 'How'ya?'

Sarah related another experience:

I was looking at my phone but it wasn't on and I saw a man's face but it was really scary. With all the stuff that was happening and waking up every night, I decided I was going to tackle this so I kept on looking at the face, making eye contact, I could see it and I said, 'Get out!' I faced him head on and said, 'You're not welcome here, leave me alone.' Ever since then that has been fine.

Sarah Jane's final experience with the unexplained took place in her bedroom.

Every night I would wake up at 3 a.m. 'cos I would look at my phone. The first time it happened I was lying there and I woke up and I couldn't move. I was petrified and I didn't want to look down 'cos I had a feeling that there was someone there and I got this overwhelming fear … It was fear!

Yvonne mentioned that there was a particular photo, again in the sitting room, and no matter what way it would be left facing, when she would return it would invariably be facing towards the window.

The lights in the sitting room would also come on for no reason. 'We have sensors that have to be operated by touch to set the lighting level and these would come on and off for no reason,' said Yvonne. Yvonne became so frustrated with this that she got an electrician out to look at the wiring. Despite his best efforts he had to admit defeat and told Yvonne that he could not fix something that wasn't broken. So whatever was affecting the lights, it would seem that it was not something that could be explained away in any conventional sense.

It was during a significant increase in the unusual behaviour of the lights that something very unusual happened.

Yvonne told how one Sunday evening she was in the sitting room on her own while her husband and son were in various other rooms throughout the house. While she was watching TV, Yvonne noticed that the small box that appears in the bottom left of the screen had appeared, as it does when you use the Sky remote to change the channel on the TV. Looking to her right, Yvonne could see the remote on the arm of the chair where she always put it and, clearly with no one touching it, the first number appeared on the screen. It was a six. Following a short pause but before the number could disappear, the next number appeared. It was another six. The same short pause followed and then the final number ... another six! This singular occurrence really caught Yvonne off guard and, with all of the connotations that come with that particular configuration of numbers, understandably so.

Having listened to the claims, my team and I returned to the house a number of days later and, having positioned the various items of equipment in the relevant locations, we gathered in the sitting room, along with Yvonne and her daughter, to begin the first investigation session of the night. As it was high summer, whatever that means in an Irish context, there was no fire lighting the room so when the lights were turned off visibility was very poor, save for the opportunity to view the events as they unfolded through the darkness by means of the night vision cameras that we were using to record the process.

Asking if there was anything or anyone unseen with us, it wasn't long before we heard knocks and bangs that did not seem to fit with the environment and, as the temperature was consistent, these could not be explained away by means of the house settling down with the contraction of timbers or the banging of copper pipes from the heating system.

Interesting enough, the house remained quiet and it appeared as if it was only on the occasions when we asked for such communication that the knocks would happen. Added to this was the observation that the knocks appeared to be coming from the direction of a particular framed photo standing on a dresser behind Yvonne, the same picture that had been discussed earlier as having the habit of changing position when no one was looking.

There is a theory that suggests that because you are trying to establish a relationship of sorts with whatever unseen presence may be there, that having the familiar face of the resident, homeowner or family member involved in the investigation can help to expedite this particular process.

Yvonne's daughter was sitting on a chair in a corner of the room and, while somewhat removed from the rest of the group, was using one of our digital recording devices and a pair of headphones to listen to what was taking place as the device continued to record. This allowed Sarah Jane to perhaps pick up on sounds and noises that the rest of the people present might miss. Experience would suggest that including the client in the process of the investigation by giving them a task helps avoid them feel like they are passive observers of something taking place in their own home. To this end, Yvonne herself was using an infrared photographic camera to take still images that might reveal something anomalous upon review later. The next anomalous noise came from near where Sarah Jane was sitting.

During set up we had placed a torch on the mantelpiece with the back rotated so that the torch was switched off but with a gentle touch it could be made to come on. It was while we were discussing the noises with Sarah Jane that the torch did just that, it came on!

This caused an immediate reaction from some of those present, making it necessary for me to point out that as we had not asked for this to happen it would be best to dismiss it as having any paranormal significance in the context of the investigation and even though any presence there had been invited to do this earlier on it was also possible to use simple physics to explain away this phenomena. One must qualify this statement, however, by pointing out that while physics can be used to explain one means by which a torch might come on, that is not to suggest that it offers the only explanation for the means by which it may come on.

However, having reset the torch we invited whoever was with us to do this again, and this time it did just that, but it is of course possible that this was mere coincidence.

Yvonne herself called out, inviting more noise to be made, and we heard sounds that seemed to be coming from upstairs, in the direction of the bedroom where reports have included the overwhelming presence of something unseen.

Sarah Jane, hearing noises in the headphones, had by this time made her way towards the kitchen area to explore further and decided, for now at least, that she had had enough of the digital recorder.

Clearly agitated by what she was still feeling, Sarah Jane returned again to the kitchen area, followed this time by two members of the team. Using the infrared camera, Sarah Jane suggested that she could see orbs passing by the viewfinder.

Some people put forward the theory that orbs may be the first stage of a spirit manifestation and notwithstanding the potential for this to in fact be true, in the vast majority of cases they can be explained away by means of dust particles or moisture in the air and in the context of a standard flash camera can also be explained away by means of the flash bouncing off of dust particles or moisture. As a number of us had walked towards the kitchen and created a disturbance, we could not discount this as a reasonable explanation for what Sarah Jane was seeing on camera.

Returning to the sitting room, there followed two reports of shadow movement seen at two different locations in the room. We explored both the movement of video cameras and the subtle changes in light emanating from the viewing screens in an attempt to evaluate if they may have been the cause, but failed to replicate this to any level of satisfaction that would allow us to consider this experience debunked.

Exploring the noises that seemed to be originating from the kitchen. (© M. Benson)

During this part of the investigation we also used a Frank's Box to explore the possibility of further communication with whatever may be present. We had not long switched on the device and invited any spirit listening to confirm their awareness of our presence by saying the name of one of the people in the room when we all clearly heard the name 'Sarah' from the device. Asking for confirmation by way of a yes or no answer, we enquired if whoever it was had in fact said the name Sarah. Immediately there came the answer 'Yes'!

'I have goosebumps all over,' commented Yvonne, having heard the comments from the device.

With her own reason for asking the following question, Sarah Jane enquired if the spirit we were communicating with was called Vincent? Again, almost immediately, the response 'Yes' came from the device. This prompted Sarah Jane to ask, 'Do you know me?' and again 'Yes … Sarah' was the response. Having heard this, Yvonne enquired if Vincent was the one who kept switching on the lights, to which the response was another 'Yes'.

Eager to know some more about his intentions at this point, Sarah Jane enquired, 'Are you good Vincent?' to which came the emphatic response, 'Yes'.

Sarah Jane took the opportunity to ask Vincent if he was the one who had been scaring her, but to this question there came no response. Asking the question did give rise to an interesting point, however, and I mentioned to Sarah Jane that frightening her may not in fact have been his intention and that moreover it was perhaps her thoughts and ideas about the experience that was making it scary, when perhaps it was his intention only to make himself known.

As we were discussing this point the surname Leddy was heard from the Frank's Box. Yvonne revealed that Leddy was in fact a family surname of some significant meaning to her. While this was sinking in everyone present heard a loud click coming from the kitchen area, as if someone was placing a glass tumbler onto the stone top on the island in the kitchen. I headed in the direction from which the noise had come and as I was making my way I enquired if that noise could have come from the ice machine? Sarah Jane and Yvonne were quick to reply that they were familiar with the sound of the ice machine and that this was a different sound entirely. Yvonne was later to inform me that this was in fact a sound that they too had heard on a frequent basis. Despite my best efforts I was unable to reproduce the sound to any similar extent as to be happy that I had identified what may have caused it. Yvonne then asked, 'Vincent, can you make that sound again?' to which the response on the box was a clear and definite 'No'!

Becoming more confident, Yvonne asked, 'Are there two men in the spirit world here with us now?' at which point the box was heard to say 'two men'. Yvonne then asked, 'Is the person related to anyone in this room?' Clear and immediate was the response 'Yvonne' through the Frank's Box. Yvonne went on to ask how this person was related to her. Yvonne was sure she heard 'Dad' in response to this question. Sarah Jane then asked how she was related, to which she heard the response 'Granddad'.

At this point, having had plenty of food for thought, we took a break before splitting into smaller groups, with one heading upstairs to explore the claims from the bedroom while the other group continued with the events that were unfolding in the sitting room.

The personal nature of the lines of questioning that followed from the first session were such that it would be inappropriate to record them here. However, the result of our investigation led to Yvonne and Sarah Jane developing a new perspective on what is happening in their home, what it means to them, why the presence is there, and in this change of perspective lies the fact that they are now prepared to coexist with it on the basis of having established their own terms and conditions – what they are prepared to accept and what they are not.

It is important to say that the reported claims of activity continue to occur at the house and, in any case, it is not our role as investigators to 'remove' a spirit from a location. In truth, on a personal level I do not believe this is possible and that if indeed there is any potential to move a spirit on to the next realm or plain of existence then this can only happen with the consent and willing participation of the spirit or entity itself.

Shortly after our investigation I asked Yvonne how things had been since we were there. 'It is like a different house really. Now that I know more I am more relaxed about it, I don't have that creepy, eerie feeling,' she said.

Any time we as a paranormal investigation team leave a location having placed the client in a more positive place with regard to their experiences it is reasonable to consider our work to be done!

5

NEIGHBOURING GHOSTS

A S is so often the case, in fact far more often than not, people who experience events such as those contained in the following account wish to remain anonymous.

For the purpose of telling this story the identity of the specific location will be withheld, except to say that it is to be found on the outskirts of Wexford Town. The identity too of those involved (with the exception of those in the Wexford Paranormal team) will remain anonymous and names changed for the purpose of recounting the events.

So what of the house itself? It is possible to walk the distance from Wexford Town to the house. This particular house makes no attempt to stand out from those around it other than to mention that it perhaps reflects the architectural tastes of the family who built it, having been built sometime around the 1980s. Unoccupied for the past number of years, this particular house has silently watched as the world passed by, people busying themselves with the ordinary, unaware of the experiences of those who have crossed its threshold or

what in the silent isolation of its currently uninhabited state may continue to prevail.

When the owner, let's call her Susan, first made contact with Wexford Paranormal she mentioned that the house was currently uninhabited by virtue of the fact that no one would stay there, such was the level of paranormal activity experienced in the house. Susan had on a number of occasions rented it out, or at least attempted to, but her tenants were quick to contact her, complaining of unexplained noises, of objects being inexplicably moved, voices in conversation being heard in otherwise empty rooms, and items disappearing only to reappear again days or even weeks later in a completely different location from where it had first been.

Susan herself had more than a few personal experiences to recount. On one such occasion Susan had cause to be staying in the house on her own as her husband was out of the country on business. On one of the nights towards the middle of that same week (Susan was unclear which night specifically), she was sleeping soundly until at some point in the early hours she was aware of a sound being made by someone in the room. Susan initially took this to be her husband returning unexpectedly from his trip. She was aware of him climbing into bed behind her and put his arm around her.

'What are you doing home early?' Susan asked, knowing that he was not in fact due home for a number of days. As she asked the question she simultaneously turned in the bed to face him, only to discover that there was in fact no one there!

'This gave me an unbelievable shock,' said Susan, 'but in truth it was by no means the first and certainly not the last unexplained experience I was to have when I lived in that house.'

Susan went on to disclose how at a previous time while she and her family still lived at the house, movement and footsteps heard coming from the upper floors were a common, if no a daily experience. She also recounted how, when her children were small, they would often spend many of their evening hours boisterously playing in the rooms on the second floor that had been converted from the attic space that it was originally. When at the end of their play the children would retire to bed on the first floor, noises and sounds of play could still be heard coming from the rooms above them, rooms that were, without question, free of any human inhabitants.

These experiences were not just the preserve of the family. Visiting friends too were by no means spared the 'pleasure' of such unexplained occurrences. One such occasion involved two friends who, while spending the night at the house, became unwitting witnesses to what they described as a full-blown conversation between presences of numbers unknown and forms unseen in the corner of the very bedroom in which they were staying. This event took place in the early hours of the morning, at a time when all others in the house had retired to bed and the rest of the house lay silent.

Another visitor to the house happened to be alone in the sitting room during the late afternoon and recalled how they were at that time admiring the long rays of the late evening sun as it entered the room, golden shards of light appearing to warm all that they touched. Distracted by their thoughts they were suddenly brought back to earth with a bump (in this case in a very literal sense) as they travelled across the room, to land on the floor following the encouraging push of a forceful but unseen hand.

I arrived at the location early on the day we were due to investigate the house in order to collect the keys, as once we returned later that evening we would be on our own for the duration of our visit – Susan had absolutely no intention of finding herself at the house after dark.

Given that the afternoon was fine and bolstered by the fact that she was not there on her own, Susan consented to a brief visit inside the house. Full credit must be given to Susan who, while clearly on high alert and putting her peripheral vision to good use, persevered long enough to go inside the location and recount again, although this time in much more condensed form, the stories connected to the house.

As Susan and I were about to leave we found ourselves back in the kitchen, a spacious and well lit area. We suddenly clearly heard what sounded very much like footsteps coming from the floors above. I hesitated for a moment and wondered if this might be in some small way an indication of the night to come … while Susan made a beeline for the door.

It was seven in the evening when The Wexford Paranormal Team arrived for the investigation proper. As we entered the kitchen we were greeted by what looked like ants with wings that had taken up residence in a window sash, to which they had gained entry through some broken glass. We brought with us the usual pieces of equipment, CCTV system and cameras, EMF meters, numerous hand-held night-vision cameras, digital audio recording equipment, motion sensors, data loggers, geophones and a thermal imaging camera. One additional requirement at this investigation was the inclusion of a generator, as there was no electricity available at the location.

Given that this house was a large detached house, eight of the team attended the investigation in order to cover more locations simultaneously while leaving opportunities for individual investigators to take breaks during the night. While eight might seem like a lot of people, it is important to say that very often these locations can be a one-shot deal so we were determined to get as much as possible from our time spent there.

With the organised precision that can only come with experience and the familiarity of working with those around you, we set about rigging the various pieces of equipment. During the set up some of the team were working in one of the hallways when they turned to see an upright piece of door surround seemingly 'thrown' up the hall. It did not just fall but seemed to travel further up the hallway. Circumstantial and even conventional reason might account for such an occurrence but it does cause you to be on your guard. CCTV cameras were positioned at some of the reported 'hotspots' around the house, the generator was located outside and far enough away so as not to be heard inside and, with power up and running, cameras were live as the team gathered for a briefing before splitting into smaller groups.

For the first session we all gathered in the sitting room to let the house settle and with everyone accounted for, we could listen to the sounds of the house and anything that did not appear to fit with convention. It did not take long.

As we sat in the silence of the enclosing night, it was possible make out the person situated to the left and right while all others in the room had fallen under the cloak of darkness and could only be seen by use of the night-vision equipment. Footsteps, or at least what sounded like footsteps, could be heard from the floor above. Not just an occasional gentle footfall but that of movement with a purpose, like someone traversing the floor above in the process of fulfilling some task or other and then returning again across the same location.

Following this we became aware of more footsteps, closer this time, coming from the long hallway outside one of the two doors of the room. Focussing our attention on the door in question, movement was noticeable. Not, 'there is someone out there' movement, just the subtle movement of shadows coming and going. Two of the team entered the hall in search of any possible cause that could explain our observances, but with a lack of windows and all other doors closed, and no potential for transient light from passing cars, we could offer no rational reason for our observations.

This session continued and with the apparent onset of activity we began to call out, asking if there was anyone unseen with us and if so to give an indication by way of a definitive noise or by speaking into one of the digital audio recorders we were using. We then asked whoever was with us to tell us their name. It is good practice to ask such questions more than once throughout an investigation, not only in the hope of capturing and answer and also a consistent response. To this end, our possible spectral visitor was subsequently asked to share their name again at a later point in the session of enquiry. Review of the recorded material some days later (after the investigation had been concluded) revealed that the name Bill was offered in response on both occasions.

As this first session continued Hollie, one of our investigators who, until now, had been sitting quietly underneath the large main window of the room, began to speak. 'Guys ... I, um ... I ... I feel like my chest has just been touched!'

Looking across at Hollie through the night-vision camera I was using I could see that she was sitting with both her knees tucked underneath her chin, with her hands clasped tightly in front across her shins. Her eyes were trained towards the ground in front of her and an expression of surprised disbelief was on her face. It was this expression that interested me most. As a team we have been in many different locations and had numerous unusual experiences but surprise and

disbelief are not two sentiments that are employed by us to any large extent.

While this was an interesting personal experience, as a team we had to acknowledge it as such, just a personal experience, and move on. Such personal experiences can never be offered as evidence, except perhaps in a situation where the experience would seem to correlate with evidence captured by other pieces of equipment, be it video or audio etc. The subsequent review of audio material in the days that followed was to certainly add much greater weight to the personal experience that Hollie had on the night of the investigation. Bill was clearly not content to just leave information regarding his name on our recording equipment. He, it would appear, was also quite eager to give explicit information with regard to his intentions. Not only did he want to inform us of what he planned to do, but also to whom he would do it. In fact, what he would appear to have said by way of what we captured on our equipment was such that I cannot in conscience use the specific words here but to paraphrase the audio that was captured, Bill said, 'Bill ... going ... (behave inappropriately) ... Hollie'. Further derogatory comments captured would suggest that he had a dislike for women generally. As we continued to discuss the experiences we were having, the words 'get out' could be heard from the kitchen area. Clearly a break was needed so we retired to the kitchen to plan session two.

At this point we decided to split into pairs for our next session and the plan was to locate these groups in noted locations around the house where specific reports have been made. Stella and Teresa headed to the bedroom where the owner had felt something in the room with her, while our tech specialist Michael and Veronica were located in a bedroom opposite on the same corridor. Breda and Carol entered the room where conversations had been heard taking place and Hollie and I headed up to the second floor, where footsteps and movement were reported on a regular basis.

This second session, which was to last one hour, was no less eventful than our first session downstairs. As Hollie and I began our enquiries, shadow movement could be seen and footsteps heard coming from the short landing just outside the door to the room we occupied. The room consisted of us, a carpeted floor and nothing else. We had left the door open to allow us to observe the space outside in the gloom while we sat with our backs to the wall opposite the door, acutely aware that were anything to come between us and the door that there was no other way to leave the room.

Again we began calling out while recording the session on a twin camera designed to be able to film from in front and behind, using a switch to alternate between the two functions. This device had also been adapted to film in full spectrum, thus allowing both the visible and invisible spectrums of light to be captured on the recording. We had also brought with us an EMF meter to capture any anomalous fluctuations in electromagnetic fields, as well as the Frank's Box.

We heard some noises that seemed to come in response to questions asked, so, for validation, I enquired, 'If you are in the room here with us can you make a sound like you made already?' No sooner had the enquiry been made when there was a loud bang, no it was more of a crash, from the floor just in

front of us and halfway between where we sat and the open doorway through which we had just come. It sounded as if a fifteen-stone man had been hanging from the ceiling by his arms and suddenly let go, falling to the floor. Such was the unusual level of noise that it caused me to respond with, 'What the **** was that?' and Hollie and I shared a surprised glance at each other.

'Why don't we use the Frank's Box for a while?' suggested Hollie. 'Did you bring it up with you?' I was sure I had but despite our best efforts we could not locate the device on the floor. 'I am sure I brought it with me,' I said. 'Shall I go down stairs and check if I left it behind?' Deciding against leaving Hollie alone in this room we carried on without it.

It was shortly after this that we both heard what sounded like a frightened outburst coming from the room below, in which Stella and Teresa were engaged in conducting their own investigation of the main bedroom. 'Should we go down and see what has happened?' suggested Hollie.

'No, let's wait to see if any of the groups on the same floor go to check them,' I replied. After all, as investigators, we are aware that every location is an unknown quantity and as a result our comfort zones, no matter how well developed for this work, can at times be tested.

There seemed to be no reaction from the other teams so Hollie and I decided to check in with Stella and Teresa, just to be sure all was ok. 'Look at that!' I said to Hollie as we stood up to leave. Switching on my torch I pointed to the floor just in front of where she was sitting. Straight in front of us lay the Frank's Box that had eluded us before despite our best efforts to locate it! 'You have got to be kidding me!' Hollie exclaimed as we both headed

'Bill' seemed to take a dislike to the women in particular. (Original artwork © Ben Hennessey)

towards the door and back down the stairs towards the room Stella and Teresa were investigating.

Entering the room, a clearly shaken Teresa informed us that she had heard what sounded like a growl in the headphones she was using to listen to the audio being recorded by the digital recorder she was using. I crossed the hallway to ask Michael if they had heard the noise only to discover that neither Michael's group nor that of the other on the same floor had heard anything, yet we had clearly heard it one floor above.

We decided it was a good time to take a collective break and headed back to the kitchen. I laid the Frank's Box on the counter next to the DVR and monitor system as three of the ladies from the team sat on the kitchen stools. Over the course of the break we were discussing some of what went on when suddenly the monitor that was illuminating the room in the darkness went off! Immediately I thought, 'Damn, the generator has run out of petrol.' I looked to my left, only to discover that the plug board that was placed on the counter top still had the red pilot light on. Thinking that the fuse in the cable to the monitor had blown we tested the cable, only to discover it was still functioning and even introducing a new cable did not resolve the issue.

After plugging and unplugging the cable into the monitor a few times I gave up and just removed it from the screen. 'It's OK guys, the DVR is still recording but we just can't see the screen,' I said as I stood with the unplugged end of the power cable in my hand.

Over the next five minutes the conversation centred on what had happened so far when Carol, who was sitting on the other side of the worktop, exclaimed, 'The monitor has just come on! … Oh wait, it has gone off again.' I replied that it couldn't have switched on but Carol was adamant. 'It did! The green light came on and the screen lit up. I could see all the cameras!'

'I know,' I responded, 'but it can't have come on'.

'What do you mean?' enquired Carol. 'I saw it come on for myself.'

No reply to this question was needed as I slowly raised my hand to reveal the end of the power cable that I was still holding. The power had not been connected to the monitor for the past five minutes! Any residual power that would have been in the transformer of the monitor would have quickly dissipated over a matter of seconds and would not have been maintained in there to allow it to suddenly switch itself on after some five minutes of being unplugged.

For the last session of the night we returned once again as a large group to the room in which we had started the investigation earlier that evening. The darkness surrounded us as we set about engaging one last time with any possible presence that resided there.

We were still one unexplainable experience away from the finish, however. During this last session, as in some of the others carried out that night, we were using our thermal imaging camera. As a group we have a policy when using this device that where possible we take infrared photos of the same subject at the same time as a safeguard against misreading or misinterpreting the captured image later during analysis. Four of the investigators present were sitting at a table in the centre of the room, all with their right hands on the table. Because the table itself had a glass top we had placed a black square of card some 40 centimetres square on the glass to prevent heat reflection being picked up by the thermal camera.

The photo we took reflected the scene outlined, but the matching thermal image showed not four hands but five! Each of the hands belonging to the team members could be matched with the photo but in addition to this was one extra hand, which, unlike all the others, was left handed and even more significant was the fact that while those of the four team members all had the same heat signature, there was a significant difference in the heat signature of the unexplained fifth hand.

To this day the house remains empty, aside from whatever invisible presence it is that has made the building its home.

6

DUNCANNON FORT

TODAY Duncannon Fort forms a picturesque backdrop for families spending sun-filled days building sandcastles and cooling off in the Waterford estuary. However, almost 500 years a fort of some description has stood here, ready to defend the area. In fact, it is possible to trace the defensive use of this location as far back as time of Conan MacMorna, who acted under the leadership of none other than that of Fionn Mac Cumhail as a member of the Fianna. They were charged with the task of defending the country on behalf of the High King from attacks from foreign parts.

Duncannon derives from Conan's Dun. *Dun* means 'ancient fort', therefore Duncannon is best described as meaning 'Conan's Ancient Fort' (Hore's *History of The Town and County of Wexford*, 1904).

The fort that we know today, or at least an earlier incarnation similar in form to that of its current structure, was first mooted as an idea back in the 1550s but it was not until 1588 that building of the fort began. Its main purpose was to defend the area from the threat of invasion from the Spanish and also to reduce the threat of piracy that was reported to have been rife in the area at that time.

By 1600 the garrison had increased in size to around 100 men, despite the continued poor operating and living conditions that the soldiers faced. Conditions continued to deteriorate to such an extent that by 1625 the poor quality and size of rations, very poor provision of suitable clothing and footwear, as well as the unpredictability of payment led to mutinous behaviour on the part of the garrison.

Between 1641 and 1645 the Confederate Catholics besieged the fort twice in opposition to English rule.

It was in fact from Duncannon Fort that Captain Ashton set sail on his ill-fated attempt to take Loftus Hall from the Redmond family, who were the occupants at that time (see Chapter 3).

The Battle of the Boyne in 1690 saw King James II depart Ireland through Duncannon Fort having been defeated

Duncannon Fort stands watchful over Waterford estuary.
(© M. Benson)

by his son-in-law William of Orange, who also arrived at the fort later that same year.

The 1798 Rebellion holds particular significance in the history of Duncannon Fort and indeed one of the more noted attractions for visitors to the fort is that of the Croppy Boy cell. Although questions still remain as to the actual location of the Croppy Boy cell, officially it is reported to be located below ground at the Casemated Battery. It is rumoured that he, along with many others, was hanged in this location for acts of treason. Croppies captured during this time would have been incarcerated at Duncannon Fort before eventually being taken to Geneva Barracks on the Waterford side of the harbour.

The tricolour flew over the barracks for the first time in 1921 and in 1986 the fort ended its days as any form of active military location.

Today the fort is managed and run by the Marion Coady, who is charged with the day-to-day running and development of Duncannon Fort as a significant historical landmark in the South East. Marion's infectious enthusiasm and passion for this location is readily apparent.

There have been many stories and reports of paranormal occurrences at the fort over the years. A number of people have reported seeing the ethereal forms of both a man and a young boy in the stone tunnel that leads towards the old iron door that exits into the

Tide and high walls ensured that access could be achieved by only the most resolute of attackers. (© M. Benson)

The old iron door that leads from a tunnel to the dry moat. (© M. Benson)

moat. A visiting sensitive/medium who reported seeing these otherworldly forms claimed that the man had been killed in battle across at Waterford, while the young boy had been taken from Waterford and been held at the fort, where he too was subsequently killed. His mother was to never learn of the fate of her son.

One local newspaper reported on an investigation at the fort by ECHO ghost hunters, who were visiting from their base in Cork. During the investigation the ECHO team reported that two of their members had something thrown after them as they made their way down the tunnel towards the Croppy Boy cell. Speaking about the experience, Emily O'Sullivan, the founder of the group, said that it felt as if something was in that space with them, something walking around. Something invisible but whose presence could be felt in every other way.

Many visitors report feeling like there are people walking behind them, only to turn around to find no one there, and of voices being heard when there is no one to be seen.

One personal experience I had happened in the middle of the afternoon one Saturday when a small number of us had returned following an investigation the night before. There were four of us in all, two from Wexford Paranormal and two cameramen who needed to get some daytime shots for a piece of work we were doing. At about 4 p.m. we were leaving the long hall and I was second from last with only John, one of the cameramen, behind me. As we passed through a doorway I turned to ask John, 'What did you say?' Being no more than eighteen inches from where I stood, John looked at me with a somewhat puzzled look and replied, 'What? I did not say anything! I thought it was you talking to me!'

There have also been reports of a skeleton being found in the wall behind the main fireplace in the Officers' Mess,

Tents were used to provide soldiers with the most basic of protection from the elements. (Courtesy Duncannon Fort)

Some of the many cannon and ammunition ready to defend the fort. (Courtesy Duncannon Fort)

with the Mess itself dating back to 1724. The caretaker's house, which stands to the left of the Officers' Mess as one looks towards it, is built on the site of the chapel that stood there before it. The floor of this present building is above ground level, in recognition of the tombs that lay beneath it. The inscription on one of these reads, 'Blessed be the hand that laid this tomb, cursed be the hand that removes it'.

Another story recounts how at one time some musicians rehearsed at the fort regularly on one evening during the week. On one particular occasion a member of this group had cause to find himself there before the rest of the members had arrived and, to occupy himself while he waited, he brought his instruments into the hall and began to tune them in preparation for the rehearsal. As he was doing this a noise began in or on the roof of the hall in which he

stood. This noise grew louder and louder until it seemed as if the very roof itself was about to be ripped clean away from the walls on which it stood. Without pausing to consider the surreal nature of this experience he promptly returned his instruments to their various cases and left the fort with a resolve never to return. To this day he never has!

As a team of paranormal investigators, we have had the opportunity to visit and investigate Duncannon Fort on a number of occasions.

One particularly experience from our first investigation relates to the underground chambers that also house the Croppy Boy cell. It was in the early hours of the morning and the mildness of the night was matched only by the stillness of the air as fellow investigator Robbie and I made our way down through the dry moat that surrounds the fort. The high stone walls on either side dwarfed us by some 20 feet or more as they framed a cloudless sky filled with vibrant stars. The rest of the team were some 500 yards away, back through the moat and beyond the parade ground in the infirmary.

We descended the stone stairs at the far end of the moat that led underground, and sat silent in the darkness as the imposing presence of the damp stone walls that surrounded us were lost from view, such was the resolute enthusiasm with which the night joined us in our efforts.

Back beyond the age-weathered stone stairs that we had previously descended stood an old sea-salt ravaged iron door that would be our access to the sanctuary of outside space. This door was in turn held open by a large stone to ensure it did not inadvertently close, its only purpose being to ensure we could in fact leave the same way.

Both Robbie and I called out, inviting any resident spirit or spirits that may be with us to make themselves known.

A laboured grating of stone on stone was heard, followed immediately by a loud bang … clang … clang! Pausing just long enough to make eye contact through the murky darkness, no spoken words were needed, both Robbie and I moved with the unspoken precision of Red Arrow pilots towards the stairs and up towards the door, fearing that someone, not knowing we were there, was locking us in!

At the top of the stairs, however, the iron door was found to be still braced open against the wall and the stone we had placed in front continued to fulfil its appointed role by keeping the door in place, right where we had left it. No other creature was visible to us as we shone our torches back along the grass carpet that lined the dry moat and with no other human being around this area, only the sound of the sea shared our experience in its own repetitive, disinterested way.

This was not to be the last time we were to witness this particular phenomenon as

Soldiers at the fort, ready for inspection. (Courtesy Duncannon Fort)

on a subsequent visit to the fort we again found ourselves back at this location, this time joined by a number of members of the public. While we were gathered in the lower cell we collectively heard the sound of stone dragging on stone, causing me to recount to the group how, on a previous visit, we had experienced the same occurrence. One of the members of the public and I headed towards the top of the stone stairs and, as was my expectation, the stone was still against the door and the door back against the wall where we had placed it. Calling down to the larger group, I said, 'I am going to try to replicate the sound. Have a listen. In three … two … one …' I grabbed the rusted door and pulled it toward me, causing the stone at the foot of it to be dragged across the stone floor beneath it. 'That's the sound!' was the immediate and unanimous response from the group below.

In October 2012, Wexford Paranormal were joined at Duncannon Fort by a team of radio presenters, Niall, Trish and Zara, from Beat Breakfast on Beat 102 103 for the purpose of recording a show for Halloween. That same week a story had reached us about a member of staff who worked at the fort. He had been down in the Long Hall and, upon entering, he saw a man dressed in full Redcoat uniform. Assuming that this person was one of the many military re-enactors who are often at the fort, he moved toward him to say hello and to shake hands with this unexpected visitor. So physically dense in appearance was this man that not a second thought was given to the situation being in any way unusual. That is until he reached out his hand to greet this Redcoat 'actor', only to find he was

alone in the room. The visitor had quite literally vanished.

Armed with this information, we decided to focus a large part of our investigation on the room where the apparition had been seen. Making our way under torchlight through the outer room of the Long Hall, we then passed through an inner hallway with the strong smell of petrol filling out nostrils as it emanated from the various mowers that were stored there. Entering the small room where the reported event had taken place, we closed the door behind us.

With torches turned off, the darkness enveloped us in a collective embrace as extraneous sounds from boats unloading at the nearby pier drifted on the air. Some of us stood while others sat, prepared to risk dampness and dust in pursuit of a comfortable position. Two of our guests on the night huddled together to temper their fear with the security of holding on to each other's arm. Robbie, who was the last of our team to enter the room, sat near the door.

Calling out to any person unseen who may have been with us in the room, we heard a 'click' coming from the door through which we had recently entered caused us to look in that direction. 'If that was you can you make that sound again?' was asked and again 'click, click' was heard, apparently in response to the question. Discussing the nature of this sound, it was suggested that it sounded like an old thumb latch. Investigating the door, we discovered that no such latch existed and indeed we were unable to reproduce the same sound no matter how we manipulated the door.

The invitation to come in and join us was offered to our invisible visitor but one of our guests called out 'No! Don't come in ... I'm freaked out!' and urgently made her way to the opposite side of the room, away from the door. 'This place is more scary to me than the other place we were in. I don't know why, it is a lot more eerie,' she continued.

Undeterred, we continued to invite this unseen visitor, if indeed there was such a person there with us, to come in and join us. At this point the door that up until now had been just making this clicking sound began to move slowly back and forward in its weathered frame. The door seemed to react to our questions and statements until it finally began to aggressively bang and bang and bang in apparent response to the encouragement of the majority group, while those less experienced threw frightened glances over their shoulders towards the door while jumping at times in synchronised response to each additional bang of the door.

Across the parade ground at the opposite side from the Long Hall is the infirmary. With such a history of injury, sickness and death this was one location we were not going to overlook. It is currently used as the museum at Duncannon Fort and claims of the sound of boots walking around the upper floor and down the stairs when there is no one else present have been reported by staff and visitors alike. On foot of these claims, one other investigator and I located ourselves halfway up the stairs in an attempt to experience this for ourselves. For some twenty minutes there was nothing to report, just the silence of the surroundings and the occasional query or observation shared between us as we debated the subject of the paranormal, thus preventing the protracted silence from becoming deafening.

'Shush! Did you hear that?' I said as I looked up the stairs into the blackness. Suddenly from the floor above us we could both hear what sounded like footsteps. These footsteps grew louder and seemed to approach the top of the stairs. Indeed not only did we hear footsteps but they had the discernible tone of a boot rather than that of a shoe and, later on, we explored the difference in tone between my boots and the shoes the other investigator was wearing for the purpose of comparison.

'Is there any other way you can let us know you are here?' we enquired. Just below us on the opposite side of the room stood a wooden four-panel screen with photos of Redcoats and soldiers while large model boats in glass cabinets adorned the rest of the room. Immediately following our question a loud bang came, as if someone had just kicked or punched the wooden panel in the room below. Such was the sheer volume of the noise that it caused us to express some expletives!

For the staff who work at the fort the most consistently active location is that of the Officers' Mess (now the Tea Rooms), where they report hearing footsteps in the building. The staff, when they are in the back pantry of the kitchen, often call out to customers upon hearing them enter, only to step out into the Tea Room to find no one there. Marion took these reports with a pinch of salt until she had her own experience of a similar nature. Marion was in the Tea Room towards the end of a working day and had just gone upstairs when she heard someone enter the Tea Room below. 'Just a minute, I will be down to help you. Please take a seat,' Marion said. Concerned with not keeping her customer waiting, Marion quickly

View from the stairs of the wooden screen that appeared to have been kicked or punched by persons unseen. (© M. Benson)

returned down the stairs and entered the Tea Room, only to find it completely empty. She'd heard no footsteps exiting the building and Marion is convinced that on this occasion she experienced what many of her staff continue to report on a regular basis.

If you visit Duncannon Fort make sure to listen out for that voice from behind and if you see a Redcoat while on your visit they might well be a member of a military re-enactment group, but then again it might be something else altogether. You might just be privy to a brief glance into events of times past, to a forgotten piece of local history, because sometimes things are not always what they seem!

7

ST SENAN'S HOSPITAL

S T Senan's hospital, just outside Enniscorthy, is as imposing as it is beautiful. Situated on an elevated site overlooking the N11, countless numbers of people have entered its halls over the years. For some it was their last place of residence, as the inconspicuous graveyard situated at the back of the main building silently attests to.

It opened in 1868 as the Enniscorthy District Lunatic Asylum for the Insane and Poor of Mind. A self-contained institution, it had on site its own church as well as bakers, cobblers and tailors. Farming also took place here, further adding to the self-sufficiency of the hospital.

If bricks and mortar can indeed absorb the energy or memory of events, then were it possible to squeeze the bricks that form this structure those memories would emanate from your closed fist as sure as water runs from a sponge.

Many stories of ghosts and spirits, of unexpected spectral apparitions as well as nocturnal visitations of departed souls and inhuman entities, come to our awareness through a friend of a friend who in turn heard it from his uncle's mother's brother. They are, by their very nature, the stuff of conjecture and inference that have invariably had layer added to layer as each subsequent teller of the story leaves his or her mark on it. For all of this, we still love them. The suspense, the perverse pleasure of allowing ourselves to be frightened, forms one of the very ties that bind every lover of a scary story to our ancestors who, sitting around the fire many hundreds of years ago, shared similar stories of the other side.

Although far more recent in their telling, the following accounts crossed my path in a strikingly similar way.

The very fact that I came to hear the following was somewhat serendipitous as both my storyteller and I found ourselves at the home of a mutual friend, enjoying a social evening that resulted in our introduction.

'So, you will surely be writing about St Senan's Hospital?' my recent acquaintance enquired, having been told that I was currently working on a book about the haunted locations of County Wexford. 'Actually, as amazing as the location looks, I am not aware of any reports of unexplained activity from that location.' I replied. That was about to change and this was the story he told me.

Winding his way through the 'sameness' that many of the drab corridors within the walls of St Senan's exude, John (not his real name) arrived at a geriatric unit that was located in the centre of the middle floor. John was a middle-aged man who had worked at the hospital for some years and it was his first evening back on duty, having been on holiday in the preceding weeks. By all accounts a very practical man, John tended to deal with what was in front of him and was not predisposed to notions of ghosts,

spirits or otherworldly visitors. His job was very much about getting on and fulfilling his role as best he could.

Heavy walls dispassionately dressed with layers of gloss paint and pitted by the rigours of time framed two rows of beds that travelled the length of the room, one down each side. At the end of this ward was a dayroom which, at night, remained locked. Beyond the dayroom lay another ward that mirrored the one in which John worked. It too had a door that entered into the dayroom from the opposite side. As protocol dictated, John new that this door would also be locked.

It was about three in the morning and John was sitting in a straight-backed chair. A single nightlight was all that was on in the dayroom. There was a window situated in the wall that separated the

St Senan's Hospital, a familiar sight as you approach Enniscorthy from Wexford. (© M. Benson)

dayroom from the ward. Behind John there was a window that looked out from the office, inside which a light was also on. All the patients were asleep and, as would often happen on quiet nights such as this, John was reading a book.

Looking up, he became aware of a patient looking in through the window at the far end of the ward from inside the dayroom, his features reflecting the light as he stood behind the glass.

John had seen this particular man on numerous occasions, as it was not unusual for him to make his way from the adjoining ward at the opposite side of the dayroom where his own bed was to look for cigarettes. This man was particularly identifiable because of his bushy grey hair.

John stood up, marked the page in his book, placed the book on the seat of his chair and made his way in the half-light towards the door of the dayroom. Unlocking the door, he stepped inside. About to question the patient's reason for being there, John looked around to discover that he was alone in the room. Stark light and a feeling of mild surprise was all that greeted him. No one else was to be seen.

Making his way towards the door of the adjoining ward, John cursed quietly, assuming that it had been inadvertently left open by another member of staff as they made their rounds. But the door was locked.

So John made his way to the adjoining ward and as he approached the nurse he said, 'For Jesus' sake would you keep Tom [not his real name] in his bed? He is after frightening the s★★t out of me.'

Sitting behind her desk, the nurse raised her head and, following a pause, responded by saying 'Well, I don't know who it was but for sure it wasn't him … he has been dead for almost a fortnight!'

John is sure it wasn't a reflection or a shadow he had seen because of the distinctive way this man used to look through the window in this manner, not to mention the singularly identifying nature of his hair. To this day John is adamant about what he saw.

John continued on nightshifts for eight weeks following his unexplained experience but he never again saw this man, or indeed the man's ghost, if that was what he had witnessed on that night.

This, however, was not to be John's only unexplained encounter at St Senan's. Some two years later, while back on nights, he was to have a second brush with the other side.

John was charged with looking after an old man who was located in the first bed on the left-hand side after entering the ward. The man was dying and as such was not expected to see the morning.

John maintained a watchful eye over this gentleman and at around 3.30 a.m. John had again settled into what may have been the same straight-backed chair he so often used and he began to read while, as instructed, maintaining his vigil next to the bed. Momentarily, however, John dozed off. Whether he slept for a minute, thirty seconds or slightly longer he is not sure. However, he awoke with a start. It felt as though someone had caught the front of his shirt and with determination pulled him out of the chair, though he could see no one.

You might imagine that it would be John's instinctive reaction to immediately check on the gentleman he was caring for. Instead, John headed down to the far end of the ward, to another man who lay in the bed furthest from where

John had been sitting moments before. To John's shock, he arrived to witness the patient drawing what was to be his last breath.

To this day John cannot explain why he left the man who was expected to die to attend a death no one had anticipated. Perhaps this dying man just wanted someone there with him. With the events of that night still as vivid now as they were then, these questions continue to haunt John to this day.

The one thing that John was very clear on, however, was that these events frightened him to the very core of his being. John prayed through the night until he returned home later the next morning. Even then he still shook, such was the impact it had on him.

John was to finish night duty a short time after and never a nightshift again.

Stories are also told of a particular stairwell in St Senan's that led from the top floor down to what was then St Brigid's Ward at the back. It was known by many who worked there that no matter what time of the night you went down there, or indeed how warm it was, the hair would always stand up on the back of your neck at this location. When rounds were done at night many of the staff would go to the wards then go back to the main stairs, go back to the wards again and return by the main corridor, such was the desire to avoid the stairwell in question. Stories circulated about an apparition that became known as the Grey Lady who would materialise at this location and in the general area. Various theories are espoused as to who she was and her reason for being there. Some suggest that she was a nurse or matron at the hospital many years ago. Reports also suggest that she has been seen by more than one person at the same time minimising the potential for it to be merely a figment of someone's overactive imagination.

John's tales enthralled me and I suspect that, were there opportunity for further exploration of the hospital or conversations with those who have worked there, one would soon discover that this presence as just the tip of a very large supernatural iceberg!

Perhaps one day we will have the opportunity to hear those stories.

8

ENDURING SPIRITS

THERE are many stories concerning Wexford's ghosts and demons, of creatures not of this world that, were it not for the diligent preservation of a small but dedicated group of people, would have long been lost to rigours of time.

While researching this book I had the pleasure of taking a walk through the backstreets of Wexford Town with Joanne Crofton, a member of Wexford Walking Tours. This walk was to introduce me to some of the Victorian stories of Wexford people and their encounters with the other side. Joanne's enthusiasm for these stories is highly infectious and one can't help but be completely drawn into the world that her words create. Although the stories are Victorian in their origins, standing at the various locations associated with them I felt as if they had just taken place yesterday.

It was six in the evening when I met with Joanne. Snow had just begun to fall and the cold acquainted itself intimately with my bones. We began our journey on the quay front just below the Talbot Hotel.

Cursed Gold

The first stop on our journey into the darker history of Wexford Town was Michael's Street, located just above the Talbot Hotel as one moves in the direction of Pierces Foundry, sadly now gone and occupied instead by a well-known supermarket chain.

Michael's Street is a row of terraced houses that are overlooked by an elevated graveyard that also backs onto Kevin Barry Street at the opposite side. There were many graveyards of this type throughout the town as, at one time, there were as many as eleven parishes in the town. Some of them are no longer there such, as the one that would have stood on the site of the present police station near Peter's Square, but many still remain dotted around the town.

At St Michael's graveyard there is rumoured to be the spectre of a Cromwellian solider, whose singular task is to guard gold purported to be buried there.

The story goes that, a dishevelled presence in a uniform weather-beaten and aged, he waits and watches to take opportunistic advantage of some unsuspecting passer-by. Should you be unfortunate enough to witness his presence he will challenge you to a duel, offering you the choice of one of two swords. One of these swords is in pristine condition while the other is rusted. Choose one of these you must, but choose quickly, as failure to do so will result in him reaching out to grab you. Should you manage to break free you would find your skin left with black marks forever evidencing his touch. However, breaking free would prove virtually impossible and his touch would be deadly, his victim succumbing to a violent heart attack.

Should you win the duel then the gold is yours to keep. The cost of this is heavy, however, as at the time of your own passing fate dictates that you remain trapped between this world and the next, defending the gold until such a time as someone else wins the gold from your now spectral form, thus freeing you to continue your journey into eternity while they assume the guardianship of the gold. It is unclear why the gold is cursed or what fate befell this solider to result in his presence at this location,

St Michael's graveyard, where the spectre of a Cromwellian soldier is reported to have been seen. (© M. Benson)

but to this day, as the story goes ... he remains.

St Martin's Eve Tragedy

From here the journey takes us once again back to the Wexford Quay and on to the new marina. Before the existence of the marina we see today, old wooden works ran the length of the harbour and small vessels as well as many tall ships docked here, filling the harbour skyline. The story here concerns a curse supposedly placed on all Wexford sailors. It is said that there was a time when Wexford sailors did not observe holy days and days of obligation. So a curse was put on them that they could not set sail on St Martin's Eve, which occurs in November. If, however, they were already at sea when St Martin's Eve arrived they were alright, but under no circumstances were they to leave harbour or set sail on this day.

Ignoring the pleas of their wives and the older sailors who implored them not to sail, every working sailor this one St Martin's Eve set out to fish the large shoals that had congregated in the waters just outside the harbour area. The boats sailed towards the breakwater and had just passed the marker beyond the ballast bank when, from out of nowhere, a storm of great viciousness arose. Every boat that had set out this day was wrecked and all but one of the sailors was lost to the sea.

This lone sailor made it back to shore, arguably more dead than alive. He was taken from the water and from there brought up to Fisher's Row.

For some days following his rescue he remained deranged and insensible. When he finally regained his senses he told of how he had witnessed St Martin on a horse riding over the breaking waves and crashing swells in the storm. Upon seeing this apparition he knew all was lost, that they would not make it back to shore again.

As he continued his recovery he became increasingly convinced that he could hear the voices of his fellow sailors and lost friends calling to him. So strong was the pull of their calls that one day, lost in abject sorrow, he walked down to the shore whereupon a wave rose up to claim the last remaining sailor who had left harbour on that St Martin's eve.

Many versions of this tale exist in both story and song and Wexford sailors to this day still will not sail on St Martin's Eve.

The Maria Reed

From Wexford Quay a short walk finds us on Wexford Bridge, where continued snowfall gives us a stark reminder of the hardships that must have been endured by the people of Wexford whose lives were sustained by the salty harvest of the sea.

It is said that on a foggy night, of which there are many in the harbour, the last of the Wexford Windjammers, called the *Maria Reed*, can be seen silhouetted against the fog as its ghostly image replays again and again its passage in and out of the harbour. The skeletal remains of this vessel are visible in the water just beyond the lifeboat hut. It is not known why this ghostly vessel is thought to be the *Maria Reed* as there are no misfortunes or supernatural occurrences associated with her during her working life.

Wexford Bridge

On Wexford Bridge back in 1798, during the Rebellion of that year, a massacre took place when ninety-eight Protestant prisoners were executed on the bridge.

One of those executed was a man by the name of William Daniel, whose remains are buried in a grave at Selskar Abbey. Reports suggest that at times the cries of those being executed can be heard from the site of the bridge which stands on the same location as the wooden one that would have spanned the river back in 1798. Many rebel leaders would have also been executed on this same bridge. At the time Wexford Town had been looked after well by the rebels until they left to go to Vinegar Hill. As they moved towards Enniscorthy and on to Vinegar Hill a man called Captain Thomas Dixon was left in charge. Captain Dixon, it would seem, was known to be a bit of a hot head and it was he who marched the Protestant prisoners out on to the bridge and he who was responsible for their murder.

As we took our leave I could only speculate as to whose cries are heard at this location and why, over 200 years later, they continue to play out over and over again the horrific tragedies of man's inhumanity to man.

The Bullring Massacre

The next stop on our journey takes us to the famous Bullring in Wexford Town and home to the Pikeman statue. Considered by some to be a hotspot of paranormal activity, the Bullring has a long and bloody history. It was at this site that Cromwell massacred many Wexford townspeople.

In 1641 Wexford rebelled and for nine years (1641–1649) held out against Cromwell and his forces. Joanne pointed out that at that time what Wexford people were supposed to be doing was protecting the coastline from attack. However, in an effort to do this, the ships went as far north as Iceland and as far south as the Mediterranean. Apparently any unidentified ship that entered the Channel was attacked and allegiances were formed with Catholic Spain. In an effort to ensure that England really knew what they were up to, Wexford people even started to fly the Spanish flag over the town.

When Cromwell turned his attention to Wexford his forces camped out at Trespan Rock, an outcrop that overlooks Wexford Town. In the wet, the cold, the fog and the mud that prevailed, food supplies within the town had been almost depleted. Expecting an attack to come from the sea, a chain had been laid across the river to prevent ships from entering and a large gun facing out to sea marshalled the harbour from its location at the mouth of the estuary. Being a shrewd military strategist, however, Cromwell sent his forces by road and while all defensive attention was focused on an attack by sea, Cromwell took the gun with little resistance.

Wexford Castle, which stood on the site of the current military barracks on Barrack Street, surrendered, whereupon Cromwell's forces turned the castle gun, resulting in the wall being breeched and forcing many Wexford people to run down to the Bullring in an attempt to escape. Unfortunately, however, at this time the River Slaney was in flood and

The Pikeman statue located in the Bullring, where four skeletons were unearthed during the installation of the statue. (© M. Benson)

as a consequence those who were trying to flee found themselves trapped between the flooded river and the Roundhead soldiers, who were by now entering the town in numbers, and between 200 and 400 hundred men, women and children were massacred.

In 1904, when excavating foundations in order to erect the Pikeman statue, the skeletal remains of four bodies were unearthed. These remains were not removed, however, and remain there today, safely ensconced underneath the statue.

The Cape Bar

On the corner of the Bullring facing the Pikeman stands the Cape Bar, which is reputed to be haunted by the ghost of a young woman who was murdered there. This woman was an assistant to a photographer who, whether drink was involved or not became a little amorous, only to have these representations turned down by his assistant. So enraged was he at being rebuked that he murdered his young assistant in a manner so violent that her blood ran out underneath the door and on to the street.

Her ghost is not the only one reputed to reside at this location, however, as it is also said to be haunted by the ghost of one of the Redcoats from the rebellion of 1798. This is not just any Redcoat, however, but that of the ghost of Lord Kingsborough, a man reputed to have brought pitch capping to Wexford and thus almost universally hated by the townspeople. Kingsborough's forces were billeted in the town. The barracks was too small for his men so his forces were given free quarter, meaning that they could enter any home in the town and demand food, fuel and lodging, regardless of whether they were welcome or not. When rebellion broke out, Kingsborough was placed in the Cape Bar, which was then a prison, and on two occasions people gathered in order to lynch him. When the rebellion ultimately proved unsuccessful it was Lord Kingsborough who accepted the surrender of the town.

Was it the surrender of the town that causes him to continue to occupy the location of what was ultimately to be a victory for him and his troops that sees him remain present at this location? Only speculation exists as to the reason for his ghost remaining at the site.

The Death Coach

From here Joanne and I continued along Main Street and I am introduced to the Death Coach! In vivid detail, Joanne describes a black coach drawn by a team of jet-black horses of the finest stock and driven by, yes, you've guessed it, a headless horseman! It is the job of this headless horseman to collect the souls from the many graveyards around the town and take them to wherever it was that their behaviour in life determined they were to go.

Years ago it was traditional for shop owners to reside in private quarters located above their shops. One such owner, known as 'Old Mags', upon hearing the Death Coach coming along the street suspected that it was nothing more than would-be criminals casing locations in order to commit theft.

Based on this assumption, Old Mags decided to stay up and call their bluff.

Ignoring the advice of her neighbours and friends, Old Mags stayed up and, hearing the sound of the carriage wheels against stone that marked the arrival of the Death Coach, she pressed her eye against the keyhole at the door to her shop. From here she could see the approach of the black coach, atop of which could be seen the cowled figure of its driver. As the coach passed her door the driver – by means of powers unknown – became aware of his observer and in one movement, both as swift and deadly as it was accurate, he took hold of his whip and lashing out struck Old Mags through the keyhole, taking her eye – but not before she first had the opportunity to see that nothing but an empty cowl sat atop the shoulders of the driver of the coach.

When her neighbours found Old Mags the following morning, her face and clothing was covered in blood, her eye was missing and her hair, which not more than one day previous had been black, had turned white with shock. Although she survived this encounter it is reported that her wits had left her. This phantom Death Coach also appears in the Disney movie *Darby O'Gill and the Little People*, starring Sean Connery.

Selskar Abbey

Leaving the Main Street, Joanne and I make our way to Selskar Abbey, which has occupied the site on which it stands since around 1190. Arguably an architectural masterpiece, its roof was sadly removed during the last century to save money, as at the time any building with a roof was liable for rates.

Here Joanne introduces me to two spectral residents, that of Alexander De La Roche and Catherine, who was the love of his life. Alexander was a Norman Lord who fell in love with Catherine, a local girl. Not much is known about Catherine except that her father rented his land for a shilling a year and, as such, her dowry was not considered to be good enough for the De La Roche family.

In order to try to get Alexander over his infatuation with Catherine, his family encouraged him to go on a crusade. There were plenty of reasons to encourage Alexander to go: adventure, the spoils of war and, perhaps the biggest motivation, the Pope granted indulgences whereby if you went on a crusade, any past sins committed would automatically be forgiven. Moreover, if you went for ten years it would be the case that any future sin you were to commit would also be forgiven and upon the time of your passing from this mortal coil you would immediately bypass Purgatory and find yourself instead going straight to Heaven.

So it was that Alexander went on crusade while Catherine stayed at home, intending to wait the ten years for his return. However, Catherine received word during this time that Alexander had been killed in battle and, in a state of inconsolable and abject despair, she became a nun. In all the twists and turns that fate can weave Alexander, it turns out, had not been killed in battle and returned to Catherine planning to marry her. Instead, he was to learn that Catherine was now in a convent and that she had taken a vow never to leave.

Devastated at this discovery, Alexander became a priest and gave all

Selskar Abbey. (© M. Benson)

his money to the founding of Selskar Abbey, subsequently becoming its first abbot.

The story as it is told goes on to suggest that Alexander and Catherine decided to wait until Judgement Day, at which time they would enter Heaven together.

A Secret Tunnel

It is widely accepted locally that Wexford Town is honeycombed with underground passageways. From the Franciscan friary it is said that one such passage leads down underneath Keyser's Lane. At one point in history (date unknown) a group of children were reported to be playing in the local graveyard of the friary (a graveyard now gone) when, purely by accident, they knocked over a tombstone only to discover it to be a false headstone designed to conceal an entrance to a tunnel.

One of the youths was a drummer and, taking his drum, he set off down into the tunnel, beating his drum to aid his progress and to alert his friends as to his progress, as they were following a short distance behind. He travelled as far as the Opera House on High Street when suddenly the beating stopped. Surprised and alarmed by the silence that enveloped them, his friends decided to return to the graveyard and wait for their friend, whom they were sure would be following close behind.

His return never transpired, however, and, fearing for his safety, the group of friends ran to the friary and told one of the friars what had happened.

In the church at that time there happened to be a Welsh miner, who offered to go down the tunnel to search for their missing friend. Returning shortly afterwards, a lamp announcing his arrival in advance through the darkness, he declared that the air in the tunnel was in fact foul and that the child must have been overcome by this foul air and, given this was the case, no one would be able to go down to retrieve his body. Reports suggest that sometimes drumming can still be heard as the boy continues to replay that journey to his death. Ironically the building in which the Fife and Drum Band now meet is mere metres from the location of this alleged occurrence.

☠☠☠

Another story concerning the Franciscan friary finds us stepping back in time again to when Cromwell attacked Wexford. In the friary he murdered some of the priests (their names are actually on one of the walls in the friary), one of whom was a newly ordained priest who had not yet celebrated his first Mass.

Many years following these events a novice priest was awoken during the night by noises in the church and, believing it to be one of the older priests, he went down to assist him, believing that he might be trying to say Mass too early or some such error of absentmindedness. Seeing a priest ahead of him towards the altar of the church he enquired, 'Father, are you alright?' to which the priest replied, 'For the love of God help me say the Mass!'

'Father,' replied the novice priest, 'it's very late at night!' but the priest merely repeated his request, 'For the Holy Virgin's love, will you help me say the Mass?'

Coming to the conclusion that neither of them was going to get any sleep until

The friary church. Do secret tunnels lead from here to the harbour? (© M. Benson)

Mass was said, the novice undertook to assist in the service. So the novice found himself giving the responses to the Mass and during this time the first light of a new dawn made its way inquisitively through the stained-glass windows of the church. Aided by this additional light the novice priest noticed as he looked at the priest that he seem to have somewhat of a shadowy form, having little in the way of any real substance.

When the Mass ended the priest gave a huge sigh of relief and said, 'Finally, now I can go into Heaven.' He went on to explain to the novice that he could not pass into Heaven until he had said his first Mass. Upon hearing this, the novice priest became really excited and implored the priest to take him with him. Refusing to take him with him at that time, the priest said, 'My son I cannot bring you with me now but I will return for you in a year and a day.'

Exactly one year and a day, the priest true to his promise returned and the novice was found that same morning having died in his sleep.

💀💀💀

As our excursion drew to a close I was eager to ask Joanne if, in all the years she has been sharing these stories and locations with visitors to the town, she herself had an experience that left her scratching her head.

Joanne confirmed that once, while travelling alone up Kevin Barry Street, which backs onto the graveyard where the ghost of our Cromwellian soldier resides, she heard a voice pass a certain comment. Looking around, Joanne found that she was on her own in the area. The particular comment had very relevant significance, to the extent that I promised not to share it, at which point we shook hands and headed for a warm and welcome coffee.

As I made my way home later I was pleased to think that in all the time spent sharing these stories of the unexplained to the many and varied visitors to Wexford Town that Joanne had an experience of her own to share, or not, as she saw fit.

9

THREE'S A CROWD

A T the risk of making a sweeping statement, there would appear to be an assumption amongst most members of the public that ghostly visitations, spectral apparitions and paranormal occurrences take place only during the hours of darkness. The following story demonstrates that this is arguably not the case and that ghostly apparitions can in fact make themselves known at any time of the day or night.

Back in 1169, Bannow Bay was used by the Vikings to enter Ireland, followed shortly after by the Normans led by Raymond Le Gros. One evening in 2005, as I made my way to visit a husband and wife who had experienced unusual and unexplained activity since moving into their idyllic country house, I pondered that much of the countryside would have looked the same as it did all those years ago, such is the unspoilt beauty of the Bannow landscape.

Lewis and Shannon had lived in their house for a number of years prior to inviting me down, in the hope that

I might experience some of the activity for myself. I had originally met Lewis and Shannon at a number of meetings I had been attending and ensuing conversations had led them to share stories of their experiences with me over coffee at the end of these meetings.

Lewis was outside tending some already well cared for flowers as I pulled into the driveway and as he made his way to the car to greet me his approach was flanked by two small dogs who, despite their size, saw it as their job to act as canine bodyguards – not that Lewis needed such an entourage as looking at him it was clear to see he could easily handle himself in most difficult situations.

We entered the house through a door that led from a small porch into the kitchen, where Shannon was busy preparing an evening meal. With greetings and pleasantries exchanged, Lewis and Shannon invited me to join them in the sitting room. We made our way down the hallway that led from the kitchen to an intersection. To the right was the stairs, underneath which they had their first encounter with the unexplained. I recall thinking that both the entrance porch and hallway were dark, despite the brightness of the day.

Following them into the sitting room, I entered what was a large space with a high ceiling formed into the apex of the roof. Located on one of the end walls was a wooden hatch that I assumed provided some additional storage space.

I was completely taken with the panoramic view of Bannow Bay that was afforded through the large window situated in the main external wall.

'Lovely isn't it?' said Lewis, 'We've never get fed up of enjoying that view. It's some of the other stuff that we are not so excited about!' His last comment reminding me of the reason why I was actually there.

'So, tell me, what has been happening?' I enquired. After glancing at each other, Lewis said, 'Things have been happening pretty much since we moved in. 'The previous owner seems to have had a fascination with figures and statues of a religious nature. For some reason they were left in the house after they moved out and therefore we acquired them along with the house.'

'We have nothing against religious statues,' added Shannon, 'but at the same time we have no desire to look at them situated around our home each and every day, so we decided to put most of them in storage underneath the stairs, by placing them in the cupboard there.'

The haunting beauty that is The Bannow landscape. It may not have looked much different when the Vikings landed over 800 years ago. (© M. Benson)

With that, Shannon pointed out of the door through which we had entered towards the stairs, just opposite.

'I assume I can expect a "Paranormal Punch line" to this?' I enquired while watching Shannon shuffle in her seat, obviously uneasy.

Lewis continued, 'We thought no more of it. We put the statues under the stairs and that was it. I can't remember exactly how long they were there but it was certainly a few days. Then one morning we came down to get something from underneath the stairs and when I opened the door the heads of all the statues we had placed there were on the floor! How does something like that happen? How can anyone explain that in a conventional sense?' I had to admit that I was at a loss to explain it in any rational way.

With attempts to apply any level of rational reason to the story racing through my mind, I was invited to follow Lewis and Shannon back down the hallway and into the kitchen. Pointing to a section of wall just to the right of a radiator, Lewis said, 'That's where Shannon sees the figure of a priest!' His tone was surprisingly matter-of-fact.

'Really?' I enquired. 'Is this something that happens often?'

'Well, he has been seen on a number of occasions and always in the same place,' replied Lewis.

I went on to explain that one of the theories regarding such occurrences is called a residual haunt, playing itself out almost like that of a movie, doing the same thing at the same time and never deviating from this pattern. Further enquiry revealed that at no point had there been any attempt to communicate on the part of the 'spectre'. This fact added to the textbook description of a residual haunt. I asked if they were aware of, or had any thoughts on why he might be here, but neither of them were aware of any background story that might have led to this. The only connection we could make as we continued our discussion was the common thread being of a religious nature between this experience and that of the religious statues.

Stepping into the space where the figure was reported to be seen, I noted that they had the heating on and the radiator was giving off considerable warmth. Despite this heat there was a cold spot immediately above the radiator and as I extended my hand to explore this, the cold wrapped itself around my arm. Tracing its perimeter, it appeared to be some two feet in diameter. 'Put your arm here,' I invited both of them, 'and tell me what you feel.'

'My goodness that's cold,' said Shannon, surprised.

Further discussion was to reveal that there were also numerous occasions when footsteps from unseen figures could be heard entering from the back door into the kitchen area and tracing their way back again from where they came.

Returning once again to the sitting room, we sat to discuss further what it all could mean in the context of some of the commonly held theories and ideologies pertaining to unexplained phenomena and paranormal investigation as we understand it in a modern context.

So far, with the exception of the cold spot I had experienced first-hand, everything else had been anecdotal. However, this was about to change. When we returned to the sitting room I had sat on a sofa immediately to the left of the door that entered from the hallway. Seated at right-angles to me on another sofa were Lewis and Shannon, both of them to the right of this same doorway. As we sat discussing their experiences and the events of the evening so far something most unusual happened.

In the apex wall above where the homeowners sat appeared what can best be described as a semi-translucent, greyish black wispy mass that exited the wall and travelled towards the middle of the room. Then, turning at a right-angle, it increased in speed and shot out through the door into the hallway before disappearing from our view. As I turned my head back from the door I immediately noticed that both Lewis and Shannon were also looking in the direction of the door, their stares fixed on the hallway outside.

As they turned towards me I asked if they had seen it. I was careful to ask the question in such a vague way to ensure that whatever answers were to follow they would not have been influenced by a description on my part of what I had seen. They both described the same semi-translucent, greyish black wispy mass that I had seen myself.

So the next time you find yourself inclined to think that ghosts are confined only to the hours of darkness, think again ... and throw a watchful glance over your shoulder, just in case.

10

MOM'S COTTAGE

IN the pursuit of material while writing this book I came to realise that, with the exception of a number of private cases that I have been involved in over the past years, I had little in the way of stories that concerned themselves with the ghostly goings on from the north of the county.

I spent a few days contemplating this fact and wondering what might be the best way to remedy this when I receive a message out of the blue from Niamh Moylan who informed me that a number of members of her family had an interest in the subject of the paranormal. She went on to say that her father could tell many stories of the local area where they lived. My interest piqued, I returned a message to enquire as to the area he was living in? The reply excited me no end. Her father lives in Camolin. A meeting was arranged. Little did I know rollercoaster of absolute enthusiasm I was about to embark.

The location arranged for our discussion was the Roche floor of Enniscorthy Castle, an opulent environment to discuss such matters as that of the unexplained and so it was that in the company of any and all the spectral residents of Enniscorthy Castle we began our conversation.

Meeting Terry Conlon for the first time, I was immediately taken by the conviction and enthusiasm with which he presented his story and, with his strong Dublin brogue, Terry made a most engaging storyteller.

My mother went to school in Camolin when she was a little girl. Eventually though she had to leave school to look after her father, my grandfather, who at the time was dying, having contracted Tuberculosis. At the time they lived in a small cottage in Camolin on Limerick Lane. In fact, it was the first cottage in a row of small cottages on Limerick Lane and many of them are still there today. This would have been around 1938 and at the time it was known as Breen's Cottage. My mother herself was born in 1919 and was married in

The old church wall where Terry and Mary sat through the night rather than return to the cottage before daylight.

1943. My father's mother came from Enniscorthy but his family were from a place called Oscar Square in Dublin.

This particular cottage was only a two-bedroomed house which, for the most part, was the norm in houses of that type at the time. The front room would have been a kitchen where all of the cooking would have been done on an open fire with great fanners in the corner. In fact, my own memory of this room is reminiscent of the label on an Irish marmalade jar that used to show the open fire and the heart, and the cat lying curled up to one side. That's exactly how it was.

My mother used to have to sleep in the back bedroom. Back then a lot more stories were shared about death warnings and one story I recall her telling me at the time that had forever stuck in her mind was to do with one such occasion when she was alone in her room when suddenly the back bedroom door opened by itself. Now, you have to bear in mind that the doors in these cottages were the old thumb latch type. This required pressing down on the latch on one side of the door and this resulted in the lever on the other side of the door being caused to rise and therefore allow entry.

However, my mother could vividly remember hearing the thumb latch be pressed down and as the latch raised the door opened by itself without anyone present at the time. A door that was slightly ajar could perhaps be opened by the wind but not one that was fully closed with such a latch on it! She could hear someone coming in and 'feel' a presence. She could feel someone breathing heavily close to her as she lay in her bed and she was

so afraid that she was too frightened to look! But she knew it wasn't a human presence, because her father was dying in the next bedroom and she always maintained that this was, without question, a supernatural experience. In fact, no one ever felt comfortable sleeping in this bedroom any time they stayed.

The cottage itself was originally owned by my grandmother's mother so our family have had a long-running relationship with the location, spanning a number of generations.

We were told this particular story as children and to be honest it used to frighten the livin' bejesus out of us! But this was not the only time this particular occurrence was to be experienced by people staying in the cottage.

Moving on a generation, there was an occasion when my wife and I came down on a weekend to stay in the same cottage. At the time my aunt was still alive and would have been the second last remaining of my mother's sisters. She was an elderly woman by this time and she had her own little bedroom in the cottage so we were able to stay in the cottage on occasion if we so wanted.

Mary, who is now my wife, and I were only going out together at the time and it would have been around 1974, some forty years after my mother's first unexplained experience. We had decided that we would come down for the weekend and stay at the cottage. That particular weekend both bedrooms were in use so there was no actual place for us to be accommodated from a sleeping point of view. So we had to sleep on the floor in front of the fire in sleeping bags, which in truth looking back was a great adventure for us really.

Now, I had never really told Mary about my mother's story as a lot of this could have been regarded as a fanciful, if not overactive imagination, but … and here is the big but … we were asleep by the fire and my aunt was in her bed – you knew she was in her bed because they were old beds and you could hear someone moving in them as they creaked if someone was to get up. Now, we were asleep – in two separate sleeping bags might I add as at that time we were being very Christian and keeping ourselves pure! The embers of the late-night fire had been stoked up and the resurrected flames that followed cast harmonious towers of dancing light around the four walls of the room.

As we were lying on the floor with the reflection of light coming from the fire when the next thing, coming from the darkened hall of the cottage, was the sound of a thumb latch opening, followed by the door actually opening!

I was lying nearest the door with Mary lying nearer the heat of the fire. As I was lying there acutely aware that the door was by now fully opened, I could hear footsteps progress steadily across the room until I was aware of them right next to my head! I could feel the presence! I could hear the footsteps! It was like slippers on lino. It was then that I could hear the breathing! Following what at the time seemed to be an age, whatever it was that had come into the room just turned around and again I could hear the footsteps as it made its way back across the room,

walked out and the door closed it again behind it, and that was it. Needless to say I freaked, totally and absolutely freaked, because I remembered the stories my mother used to tell us all those years ago!

I alerted Mary and told her what had happened so we both got up and left the house, my aunt was still in bed; in fact, we didn't disturb her at all as we very carefully left the house. From there we went to the home of another remaining aunt of mine and tried to gain entry by knocking on her door, but she too was in bed and did not respond to us, despite our best efforts. We were so scared at this stage that we ended up sitting on the old stone wall of the Church of Ireland church in Camolin until daylight found us because we were so scared. So scared, in fact, that we would rather spend time in close proximity to the many old headstones that occupied the grounds of the church than attempt to return to the sitting room of my aunt's cottage!

A number of years passed and I happened one night to be in a pub in Camolin, a venue that I always knew as Jack Mac's, where I was sharing a drink with a cousin of mine. During the course of the night my cousin happened to introduce me to the man who had by now taken ownership of the cottage. During our conversation the new owner happened to mention that one of his children was sleeping in the back bedroom and this prompted me to ask if, by any chance, anyone had ever experienced any strange occurrences or phenomenon in this room. This question, while offered innocently enough, caused the man to round on me, to the extent that I was so

The view from the Bann Bridge, where the sounds of battle were heard.

taken aback that I walked away from the conversation.

However, later that night this man came back over and said, 'Look, I'm sorry I got so nasty with you, but just to let you know we did have unusual experiences in that room and we can't get one of our children to sleep there at all!'

Even though the cottage had been sold, our affection for Camolin was such that we still tried to get back to visit as often as possible. My wife and I decided to return one particular weekend and on this occasion we decided to camp out near the Bann Bridge that cross the Bann River on the Gorey side of the village. That turned out to be a most unusual event altogether because at some point during the night we were exposed to what I can only describe as the sounds

of a full battle. Now, it is widely known that many battles took place in this area during the Rebellion of 1798 and I also know that it could be argued that some of what we heard could be explained away as the cry of a fox or vixen. But I know what the cry of a vixen sounds like and this was different. We could hear the muffled cries of humans! We could hear the thunderous sounds from the hooves of charging horses! There was the distant sound of cannon fire!

I took my torch and, switching it on, I exited the tent to see what was going on. There were no visible horses, cattle, sheep or even any wild animals to speak of but still all of the sounds that had begun while we were in the tent continued unabated all around me!

I mentioned this to an uncle of mine as he was familiar with the history of the area. Even as I did so, a huge part of my mind remained sceptical as to what I had experienced. That was of course until he went on to tell me how there are numerous accounts of reported encounters with the spectral re-enactment of battles from 1798 and that they were always witnessed during the summer months of June and July. There were four of us in the tent and we all heard the same thing at the same time …

So Camolin, it seems, has its own significant contribution to make to the paranormal fabric of County Wexford's haunted history. If you should ever get the chance, why not visit the Bann River some late June or July evening, and as the rising mists of early evening begin to assert their dominance along the banks of the river, you too just might bear witness to a land that has not just soaked the blood of battle but the very memory of the battles themselves and when the opportunity presents make you the next unwitting witness!

11

IN WILTON'S SHADOW

WILTON Castle, located just outside Bree, has a reputation for being haunted. The ghosts reputed to haunt the location are three in number and while they include a magistrate and an actress, the most prominent has to be that of the ghost of Colonel Harry Alcock. The castle has been in the possession of the Alcock family and used as a family home since 1695 and Colonel Harry Alcock inherited the property in 1840. During his time in residence he carried out some repair and restoration work on the property and is credited with the construction of an additional square tower built from granite taken from mount Leinster. During the civil war in Ireland, the property was reduced to a shell following an arson attack on 5 March 1923.

Legend has it that each year a phantom coach pulled by a team of spectral horses makes its way from Wilton Castle, carrying the body of Harry Alcock to his final resting place. So dependable was the occurrence of this particular apparition that people would gather to witness the event.

These are the well-documented events and reports from the location, but what other encounters with the afterlife have people experienced in this area? What lurks behind the shaded windows of the less conspicuous buildings that lie in the shadow of Wilton Castle?

This is the story of one such house, and these are the experiences of one family …

Nestled in the shadow of Wilton Castle is a bungalow. This bungalow was built about fifteen years ago and is just like other buildings of that era.

Jim and Trina, the owners of this bungalow, live with two of their children under the watchful gaze of Wilton Castle. Joining them in their dining room, Jim and Trina sit opposite me as the youngest of the children drifts past the door casting glances of dispassionate curiosity towards me. Both Jim and Trina are musicians but they never considered themselves to be 'in tune' with these types of occurrences.

Taking a sip from his mug of tea, Jim placed the mug on the table as he began his story. 'The first experience had to be the saga in the sitting room,' he said, as he glanced towards Trina.

We had a funny thing going on where the TV used to change channels, switch itself off, go on standby, come back on and change channels again without anyone near the controls. I actually put this down to a problem with the system until a friend of mine was here in the house one day and he was actually laughing about the whole thing. So I turned on the TV and said to him, 'Here, you take the controls and put it on a channel.' My friend was about to say that there was nothing wrong with that but before he could finish the sentence it again changed channels itself.

Joining the conversation Trina reminded Jim what they had noticed in the corner of the room.

We also had shadows in the corner of the sitting room, in the right-hand corner as you come into the sitting room. Then we had a situation where Trina was playing with the Wii and I was sitting in the corner of the room watching. Now I wear a chain, always have, and as I was watching Trina this chain was lifted from my neck. I almost felt as if it was played with. I absent-mindedly said, 'Ah, stop. Go way will ya?' Until it dawned on me that there was no one behind me.

Jim went on to mention a wooden press with glass doors that stood in the corner of the sitting room. In it were numerous drinking glasses with names on them and Jim said that this press was always kept locked. Despite this, he would often come in to find that the glasses had been moved about inside the press. Enquiring if he had seen them move, Jim admitted that neither of them had actually seen the movement but given that they keep it locked they are at a loss to know what reasonable explanation could be offered for this strange occurrence.

'On another occasion I was standing in front of the fire and I was giving out to the kids for something they had done outside in the yard. Now I can't say I stumbled, I can't say I fell, but I felt as if I was pushed from behind,' said Jim.

For a period of time that seemed to bring events in the sitting room to an end but according to Jim and Trina this was only because the activity seemed to move to the bedroom at the bottom of the hall.

'The bedroom seems to be the most active location, even still,' said Trina.

Every night you get into bed and just as you are dozing off you hear two loud bangs or cracks and they really do make you jump, that's how loud they are. The odd thing is that even though we both hear it, Jim thinks the sound comes from his side of the room while I can clearly hear it occurring on my side of the bed and very close as well.

'We started getting brave then,' Jim added. 'We would sit up in bed and ask "What do you want? What's going on? Who are ya?" And stuff like that. We don't get any answer.'

Notwithstanding the possibility of a rational explanation, I offered them the theory that given that it is the same sound, and is repetitious by nature, it might be what some people refer to as a residual effect and as such has no intelligence of its own – if this is the case then it cannot answer their questions.

Jim did not always need the TV remote to watch the channels change. (Artist's impression)

'There was a gemstone that I used to keep on my dressing table,' Trina interjected.

We just woke up for some unknown reason. Light was shining in from the hallway through the open door and in the half-light we could kinda see the stone fly right through the air and land right at my feet at the end of the bed. I picked it up and it was my stone. We just looked at each other and, well … I won't repeat what we said!

'That really frightened me!' added Jim. 'I got up and turned on the light. It was the first time I ever saw anything move by itself with no one there!'

Trina went on to mention that she needed little excuse to spend some time shopping and on one such occasion she returned from a shopping trip and, entering to her room, hung two bags containing clothes she had bought on the handle of the wardrobe. They remained hanging there for the rest of the day and were still there as Jim and Trina settled down for the night.

> I was settling into sleep, or I had dozed off and woke up and we could hear the bag gently moving, like someone having a peek in the bag! Then the rustling stopped and whatever it was must have moved across to the next one because we could hear the other bag moving. I mean it sounds harmless but how can you say there wasn't someone having a look in the bags? If that had been on the floor I might have thought it was a fashion-conscious mouse or something but not when they were hanging there and especially for the length of time they were.

Trina's stories of the bedroom location continued:

> There is something about that room that I don't like! Put it this way, I don't think they like Jim. There is always some noise, a bang or Jim might feel something touching his feet at the end of the bed. One night we were in the bed and Jim felt something coming up between us from the bottom of the bed and underneath the duvet.

Trina was clearly finding the recollection of these events uncomfortable and long periods of silence were frequent. Trina continued:

I have had other experiences as well. Let's just say that at times it seemed like there was an agenda of physical engagement from whatever it was that was there but we could not see.

Trina went on to mention that when all this started it was frightening as they had no idea what was going on, and even wondered if they had done something to cause it in some way. 'It was the thought of something being there that you can't see and, if we can't see it, what's it gonna do to us?' she said.

I mentioned that people often report a connection between any recent renovations to a house and the beginning or an increase in unexplained activity. Trina told me:

> There was one morning I was here and it was back in winter. I was here on my own, lying on the couch, when the sitting room door opened fully on its own! That freaked me out alright, 'cos it just opened as if someone was coming in but there was no one there. There was no draught in the house that would have caused it and if there was, wouldn't it happen frequently as a result? We have also witnessed the red and yellow go-cart that we have outside move back and forward across the patio.

Trina went on to tell about how one night Jim was sitting up in the kitchen with the hallway door open, while she herself had gone to bed, when he saw a woman with blond hair and wearing a white old-style nightdress. Jim at first thought it was Trina messing about with her blond hair extensions so, going down to the bedroom, he asked Trina why she

The tractor, it seems, had been thrown from the shelf and knocked to the ground. (Artist's impression)

was putting in her hair extensions? Trina responded that she wasn't and, still thinking she was winding him, up he lifted the duvet cover to catch her out wearing the nightdress he had seen her in. The only problem was Trina was not wearing a nightdress at all; she had a pair of pyjamas on! Somewhat surprised at his behaviour, Trina asked what was going on. Jim then told her about the blond-haired woman in the nightdress. This apparent apparition had just come down the hall, peeped in around the door of the room and looked at him before turning and heading back down the hallway.

We also hear footsteps in the hallway and sometimes it even sounds like whoever it is uses a walking frame ...

because you can hear the click of the frame on the floor, then the shuffle of feet, then the click of the frame again. Sometimes they are nothing more than partial apparitions, a leg bent at the knee, an arm, a hand or hair then it is gone again.

One Sunday morning we were in the house on our own as the kids were staying elsewhere. It was about 5 a.m. when suddenly we heard this unmerciful crash in Brandon's bedroom! My immediate reaction was to think that Bella, our dog, had been left in that night and that she had somehow got into the room.

When we came down to Brandon's room, however, there was no dog, no one else in the room or in the house. All that greeted us was one of Brandon's large metal toy tractors lying in the middle of the floor, broken into pieces.

Trina showed me where the tractor had been kept on the shelf. 'Jim built those shelves himself especially for the tractors that Brandon collects,' she said.

Jim's first thought was that perhaps the shelves were off level and that the tractor had simply rolled off and fallen on to the floor. He checked to see if this was the case but the shelf was fine. It was not off level. Even if it had been, the tractor would not have travelled as far as it did by just rolling off.

We did have a paranormal investigator come in some time ago to check out the place and he said that there was definitely something in the room and looking to interfere with the family. He also indicated that this 'thing' was attempting to come between us.

Our youngest girl was in the bath one day and I had gone down to the kitchen to get a glass to wash her hair off when I heard her say, 'Go away from me!'

I went back up and she said, 'Mom, I want to get out of the bath now.'

Trying to just ignore it, I told her she had to have her hair washed off but she insisted, 'No, because that fellow keeps looking at me!'

I thought, oh no, what are we dealing with now? As I took the towel to dry her she said, 'He is looking in the window Mammy!' but I couldn't see anyone.

Trina told me that it was one thing for the adults to be aware of what was happening but as they had never spoken about it in front of the children it was a real concern to hear one of them speaking like this.

Jim told me how two guys were heading down the lane that runs beside the house in order to check on some sheep during lambing season and came across what they described as a 'tall man' walking towards them from the opposite direction. They said hello to the stranger. He, however, did not talk back! He just continued past them and as he did they turned to look at this person who had completely ignored them only to discover that he had totally disappeared!

This figure was seen a second time. On this occasion he was again at the bottom of the lane but this time one of the people who saw him actually went over to him in an attempt to make conversation. As he approached, the figure vanished right in front of him.

The general consensus from those who are aware of these particular sightings is that the 'tall man' must be the ghostly apparition of one of the staff who once worked on the grounds of Wilton Castle. This man is reported to have stood some 6ft 6in or 6ft 7in tall and strong in stature.

'We have our own experiences of something similar in nature from our house as well,' Jim added.

We call him the 'Hat Man' and he was seen here on two occasions, once by my second son and one of his friends who was staying in his room. His room was illuminated by a rope light that he had set up. He was about fifteen at the time and thought this was a very cool thing to have. This very tall figure of the Hat Man appeared and walked up between the two beds, my son in one bed and his friend in the other, before disappearing.

My son took to screaming. Now, I was in bed and I heard the scream.

It was such a high-pitched and fearful scream coming from a fifteen-year-old chap, that my first thought was that he had in some way seriously injured himself. By the time I ran up to the room and opened the door there was nothing there and my son was literally trembling.

Having given this figure the title of the 'Hat Man' Jim could not believe it when I informed him that there are reports from all around the world of sightings of such a figure. Always described as very tall and wearing trench-coat-style attire and a flat brimmed hat, he is often reported as standing, just watching or observing, before disappearing.

Jim continued:

He was seen on the second occasion outside the window by my sister, her daughter, one of my sons and one of his mates. He had no features, for all intents and purposes, with his hands in his pockets and just looking in. They couldn't identify a nose, face eyes … nothing! This was at about ten or eleven at night and one of the guys ran outside the house, thinking there was someone, only to find the outside empty and devoid of any other living person. He thought this was someone who knew us or someone who was coming in as the house is always fairly busy, there is always someone coming or going. With the distance from the window to the nearest point of outside cover, no one could have managed to hide in that space of time.

Eager to know the history of the location, Jim had undertaken his own research as he was interested to know if a previous dwelling that may have stood on the site would in some way go towards explaining these events. He discovered that back in the 1700s the land was subdivided for tenants who would have raised their own crop on these sites while working for the owner of the castle in return for the right to use the land. It is reasonable to assume that dwellings of some sort, however makeshift, would have occupied the area and possibly this very location. In fact, Jim pointed out that a well that would have serviced the tenants of the area was located in a field just behind their house and that this was only filled in in very recent times – certainly within living memory.

Jim concluded by telling me that he and Trina had gone through a range of emotions from 'That's it, we're selling the place!' to 'This is home. Why would we want to be anywhere else?'

So, for now, the family continue to live in the bungalow and the occurrences continue to take place.

12

A BARREL OF LAUGHS

TIME and time again, people use belief as the fundamental cornerstone of all they espouse or accept in matters of the supernatural or paranormal. It can be argued that when belief is at the root of such things that this causes a person to form assumptions that influence perceived experiences.

Belief on its own therefore is not a sound basis for the argument that something exists. There needs to be more. Considered opinion, questioning, testing and re-evaluating will all ultimately add weight, value, substance and conviction to the nature and, dare I say, truth behind any experience you may have had. The following story illustrates this point.

Back in the early 1980s, when Ireland was in the grip of 'Moving Statues' fever, Michael was an enthusiastic fifteen-year-old who had discovered the many positives that having a girlfriend offered.

He had made the assumption that discretion was the better part of valour and had not yet seen fit to inform his parents of the developing relationship. So, instead

of telling them that he was off to spend the evening with her, Michael pretended that he was heading to Rocklands, where others had gathered to observe the statue there.

Michael's girlfriend lived on the old road that ran behind the County Hospital and on towards the Ferrycarraig. When he got to the house, he was told that his girlfriend was not there; she had gone to visit her friend but that he was to call over to see them.

The friend she was visiting lived back past the hospital, on the road near the racecourse. Eager to get there as quick as he could, he had decided to take a shortcut that would take him through a wooded area along the perimeter of the hospital.

It was almost dark and the wind was getting up. When he arrived at the edge of the wood, the branches on the trees were waving to him, inviting him to come in – or were they were actually waving him away? Given the increase in distance and time involved in going by the only alternate route, nothing was going to stop him taking passage through the woods.

Entering the wood and advancing along the perimeter of the hospital, all sounds of road traffic and the coming and going of the world in general left him, to be replaced by the sound of leaves rustling on their branches, talking perhaps about this stranger in their world.

As he reached the middle of the wood, something, and to this day he does not know what, caused him to look to the right and back towards the direction from which he had just come. What he saw caused him to momentarily freeze in absolute terror! As he looked through the trees, he could see a figure, a hooded, caped figure, dressed in white and hovering some 6 or perhaps 8ft above the ground. Gathering himself, his mind still reeling, he quickly turned towards his intended route and, whistling to try to ease his fear, accelerated his advance towards the safety of the road.

Finding that he was back on the road by the racecourse, his terror eased somewhat, and he felt the comfort of other people being 'normal' as they passed him on their evening walks.

Replaying again in his mind what he had just seen, he arrived at the gates of the house and was greeted by a black-and-white collie dog whom he had met on many previous visits to this house. He put his hand down to acknowledge the dog, as he had done many times before, but the dog, instead of engaging him with friendly willingness, started to snarl and growl and back away from him until it disappeared behind the side of the house.

Michael spent a sleepless and uncertain night, convinced that he had been followed by something unseen after his encounter in the woods.

The next day he could still not get the event out of his mind. Rather than allow it to consume him, he decided to return to the location, during daylight this time, to try to come to terms with what he had seen, to face his fear.

Retracing his steps in reverse, he entered the woods from where he had exited the night before. Tentatively, he approached the location where he believed he had seen the ethereal form. He found no ghost. Instead, standing at the edge of the wood, was a large black circular 1,000-litre oil drum, raised from the ground some 6ft by three concrete block pillars. The ends of the drum had been painted white and looking at the end of the drum through the trees gave it the impression of having a hooded human form.

Had he not decided to return, he would have forever believed that he had a brush with the other side.

This story demonstrates the importance of a considered questioning of things. Not for the purpose of living life as a doubting Thomas, but to add substance to the validity of your experience.

First ask yourself what you think you are seeing, and then ask yourself what you are actually looking at, because seeing is not believing when what you believe influences what you think you see.

Also from The History Press

More spooky Books

Visit our websites and discover thousands of other History Press books.

www.thehistorypress.ie
www.thehistorypress.co.uk

The History Press Ireland